THE CAPTAIN'S CODE: 7 LESSONS TO SUCCESS, HAPPINESS, AND SPIRITUAL AWAKENING

A SELF-IMPROVEMENT GUIDE TO FINDING PURPOSE, HAPPINESS, BUILDING EMOTIONAL RESILIENCE, AND REDEFINING SUCCESS

AF520307

CAPT. UTPAL HALDAR

Clever Fox® PUBLISHING

Chennai • Bangalore

CLEVER FOX PUBLISHING
Chennai, India

Published by CLEVER FOX PUBLISHING 2025
Copyright © Utpal Haldar 2025

All Rights Reserved.
ISBN: 978-93-7500-452-3

This book has been published with all reasonable efforts taken to make the material error-free after the consent of the author. No part of this book shall be used, reproduced in any manner whatsoever without written permission from the author, except in the case of brief quotations embodied in critical articles and reviews.

The Author of this book is solely responsible and liable for its content including but not limited to the views, representations, descriptions, statements, information, opinions and references ["Content"]. The Content of this book shall not constitute or be construed or deemed to reflect the opinion or expression of the Publisher or Editor. Neither the Publisher nor Editor endorse or approve the Content of this book or guarantee the reliability, accuracy or completeness of the Content published herein and do not make any representations or warranties of any kind, express or implied, including but not limited to the implied warranties of merchantability, fitness for a particular purpose. The Publisher and Editor shall not be liable whatsoever for any errors, omissions, whether such errors or omissions result from negligence, accident, or any other cause or claims for loss or damages of any kind, including without limitation, indirect or consequential loss or damage arising out of use, inability to use, or about the reliability, accuracy or sufficiency of the information contained in this book.

CONTENTS

ABOUT THE AUTHOR

Captain Utpal Haldar is a Master Mariner with over three decades of experience in commanding some of the world's most sophisticated ships across international waters. A lifelong sailor, scholar, and mentor, he has spent his career not only navigating oceans but also guiding young mariners through the deeper currents of life. His mentoring goes beyond nautical charts, embracing the timeless wisdom of the sea to teach principles of resilience, leadership, and purposeful living.

A Master of Science graduate in Marine Operations Management, Captain Haldar has been involved in maritime research, ship safety systems, and crew development. His passion for learning never anchors — he continually upgrades his knowledge, exploring new technologies and trends in the ever-evolving shipping industry.

The Captain's Code is a distillation of hard-earned lessons from stormy decks and calm horizons alike. Through vivid storytelling and sea-borne metaphors, he offers a navigational guide not just for seafarers, but for anyone seeking a richer, more meaningful life.

Today, Captain Haldar continues to mentor, write, and inspire — proving that the sea doesn't just make sailors; it shapes thinkers, teachers, and timeless storytellers.

CHAPTER 1

SET YOUR TRUE NORTH — DEFINE WHAT A RICH LIFE MEANS TO YOU

Part 1: The Rescue and the Compass Within

The Night We Fought the Tide

IIt was supposed to be a routine evening. (quick suggestion: I should be near t not our)

Our ship had just docked at a US port. The air carried that unmistakable bite—crisp, cold, and smelling of metal and salt. It was early winter, and the water temperature was around 5 degrees Celsius—cold enough to numb your fingers within minutes. The daylight was fading, and a soft shadow began to fall over the port. It was just another ordinary day—or so we thought.

Then the call rang out: "**Man overboard!**"

That moment changed everything.

A deckhand, one of our crew members, had slipped while working on the crane. He had fallen into the narrow space between the hull of our ship and the wooden wharf. The gap was small—barely a few feet wide. It was the worst possible place to fall, a dark trap between metal and wood piling, where cold water surged violently with every small wave.

He was there—in the freezing water, wedged in that gap.

The shock of the fall and the icy water hit him all at once. He didn't scream much, just a few gasps. That's what cold water does—it numbs your body, it steals your voice, your strength, and eventually, your life.

The crew responded immediately. I was on the bridge, but within seconds, I was running down. Flashlights, ropes, radio calls—all in motion. Some crew threw life rings; others scanned the water with spotlights.

He had just minutes.

In 5-degree water, hypothermia sets in quickly. Muscles freeze, lungs struggle, and a man who could swim in a warm pool might not even float in cold water.

We found him struggling, pinned, and drifting toward unconsciousness.

Seven minutes to be exact, with the help of some agile crew and dock workers, we pulled him out, soaked, shivering, broken. His pelvis was fractured, and he screamed in pain once he recovered from the water. But he was breathing. Alive.

We rushed him to an ambulance. As I stood watching the flashing red lights disappear down the road, I felt something shift in me.

We had just saved a life.

And that moment, I felt richer than any wealth I had ever earned.

A Wealth That Money Can't Buy

There's a kind of wealth that doesn't fit in a bank account.

That night reminded me of it.

No amount of money could have replaced the sense of purpose, pride, and unity we felt. We weren't heroes. We were shipmates—each one stepping up when it counted. And in that moment, I understood something deeper than all my years at sea had ever taught me.

A rich life isn't measured in terms of money but in depth.

That's where this book begins—not in the pursuit of wealth, but in the understanding of *richness.*

Part 2: Finding Your True North — What Are You Sailing Toward?

The Captain's Compass

At sea, when navigating, nothing matters more than your compass.

Not the size of your ship, not the power of your engine, not even the condition of the sea—if you don't know where you're going, you're just drifting.

Our sailors' lives are guided by one principle: **Find your True North.**

It's the unwavering point on your compass that keeps you aligned, especially when the sea is rough and the sky is gloomy with threatening clouds. Even when every visible sign disappears—no sun, no stars, no land—you still have that needle, pointing you back to what matters.

In life, your *True North* is your **purpose**. It's your reason for waking up. It's the internal compass that guides your choices, helps you steer through challenges, and makes your journey meaningful and memorable.

Without it, life can feel like a vast ocean with no port in sight.

The Illusion of the "Perfect Destination"

When we talk about Richer Life, many people think happiness is a destination—like one day, when they earn more, retire early, buy a dream house or a dream car, they'll be "rich."

But I've seen people who had all those things and still felt poor inside.

And I've seen deckhands with barely any possessions but full of joy and purpose.

So, what makes someone truly rich?

It's not the size of their ship; it's the direction of their sail.

True richness comes from:

- Knowing who you are
- Being proud of what you do
- And feeling peace at the end of the day

Money is important in life, and that's why we work, but it's not the end of the world.

Your Life Chart: Drawing the Route

As a captain, I cannot imagine starting a voyage without a passage plan.

We chart our course based on the destination, distance, weather, current, and obstacles like fixed objects, shallow water, etc. We review the map again and again. We even have alternatives and backup plans in case something goes wrong.

But how often do we do that in life?

If I ask you:

- "What is your True North?"
- "What makes your life meaningful?"
- "Where are you really heading to?"

Most of you will pause or shrug. Maybe the answer is unknown.

That's dangerous—it is not about the sea, it's about life.

So, here's your first task as the captain of your own life: **Find your True North and chart your course.**

Ask yourself:

- What brings me joy?
- What would I do even if I weren't paid for it?
- What legacy do I want to leave behind?

When you answer those questions to your inner self, you begin to find your **True North**.

Part 3: The Captain's Perspective — Riches Beyond Gold

The Ship and the Soul

A ship can be newly built, equipped with the latest systems, and painted in dazzling colors. But if her compass is broken, if her hull is rusting from the inside, or the engine fails to start, she's not seaworthy.

Human lives are the same.

You can wear fine clothes, hold a top position, and still feel lost. Or you can live simply, with contentment, meaning, and relationships that anchor you. That's real richness.

I've often reflected: what makes some sailors glow with life while others feel like they're just enduring it?

The answer, more often than not, lies in what they're chasing.

Some chase **position**. Others chase **peace**.

Some chase **income**. Others chase **impact**.

Some chase **things**. Others chase **the truth**.

The ones who feel rich aren't necessarily the ones with overflowing bank accounts—but those with **a full heart, a clear conscience, and meaningful connections**.

I remember a senior officer I sailed with early in my career. He was known for his discipline, efficiency, and the ample income he commanded. But behind closed doors, he was bitter and restless. He complained often about family misunderstandings, his loneliness, and his failing health. One evening, as we stared into the sea after a long shift, he said something I've never forgotten:

"Captain, I spent my whole life chasing wealth, and I'm not sure I ever lived."

He had financial assets, yes. But *life assets*? Those were in short supply.

That's when I began to understand the real difference between **being wealthy** and **being rich**.

The Richness in Moments, Not Materials

There was a time, during an arrival in one of our ports, when the pilot arrived for berthing at 6 PM. That was a long pilotage through Puget Sound. The old senior Pilot mentioned that it was his Birthday, but he would not be able to complete the job and celebrate his Birthday with his wife and family. By the time he reaches home, it will be past midnight. Pilotage and berthing are crucial operations, and nothing we can do except wish him a Happy Birthday. But it kept on bugging me that he would miss his Birthday, and for the next one, he had to wait for one more year. I made a quick call to the Chief Cook and informed him of the situation. It was his off-duty hours, but the cook was so touched that he quickly baked a small cake and made little decorations on top. Around 5 hours later, when we reached the port, we surprised the pilot with the cake, and we celebrated his birthday in the middle of nowhere. No party halls, no cake shops—just a mess room, a homemade sponge cake, and laughter echoing in every corner of that metal hull.

That night, as we sang birthday songs, I saw something beautiful—**joy without luxury, connection without condition.**

That's richness.

It's in:

- A safe return home after months at sea
- A letter from your child waiting on your bunk

- A joke shared in the engine room
- A life saved in freezing water, as I shared earlier

Those are the richness that don't depreciate.

The True Ledger: What You Really Carry Ashore

Each time I leave a ship and head home, I reflect: *What have I carried back?*

- New friendships?
- New lessons?
- Peace of mind?
- Memories that made me feel alive?

If the answer is yes, then I've returned richer.

If all I've returned with is exhaustion, pay, and regret, then I've gained little.

Ask yourself:

- What will you carry with you when your journey ends?
- What will people remember you for?
- What wakes you up in the morning with purpose?

That is your richness.

Part 4: What Does "Rich" Mean to You?

Learning the Meaning of "Rich" at Sea

Back then, I was a junior officer. One night, after my watch, I went to the galley and found our Mess-man—Alberto—sitting alone, eating dinner. He smiled and offered me a seat. I was tired, but something about his calm presence made me sit.

Alberto had no rank. No fancy uniform. He earned a fraction of what I did. But as we talked, I realized how content he was. He spoke about his small farm back home, his two daughters, and how every salary he sent brought change to his family and his village. He beamed with pride—not for anything he owned, but for what he *gave*.

That night, he said something that has never left me:

"I may not be rich in money, but I sleep well. I laugh. I'm at peace. Isn't that enough?"

I nodded, and later, as I stood alone on the bridge, staring at the vast, endless water, I thought—*Who is truly rich here? Me or Alberto, with his joy and inner stillness?*

What Richness Feels Like

Richness is watching your crew celebrate a safe voyage after the safe delivery of cargo.

It's calling home after weeks at sea and hearing your child's voice say, "I miss you, Papa."

It's standing at the bow of the ship during sunrise, the whole ocean glowing in front of you, and feeling like you belong to something infinite.

It's knowing that someone's life, like the young crew who fell between the ship and the wharf, was saved because your crew acted fast. Because *you* were there.

That kind of richness can't be bought. It can only be lived.

Your Personal Definition of Richness

Now, dear reader, I want you to pause for a while, close your eyes, and ask yourself:

What does "rich" mean to you?

Is it a number?

Is it a feeling?

Is it freedom, or impact, or joy?

Only you can define it. But I invite you to expand your definition.

Try this short reflection:

- What's something you do that brings joy, even if no one pays you for it?
- When did you last feel *truly alive*?
- Who makes you feel like you're enough, just as you are?

The answers may surprise you.

"A rich life is one where your compass points to meaning. Where you have direction, peace of mind, people to love, and stories worth telling."

The cargo of such a life isn't measured in metric tonnes—it's measured in memories, values, and inner fulfillment.

Part 5: Poverty Isn't Always About Money

What Defines Poverty? What Defines Wealth?

Many people think poverty means having less money. But I've seen rich men bankrupt in terms of **time**, **health**, and **peace of mind**.

Here's how I define these terms:

- **Poverty** is not just the absence of money, but the absence of meaning, love, direction, and freedom.
- **Wealth is not just about income—it's about influence, integrity, insight, and inner calm.**

When a sailor is lost at sea without a compass, chart, without bearings, he is poor—regardless of the ship he's on.

When a sailor knows where he's headed, even if his ship is small and old, he is rich.

When we hear the word "poverty," our minds immediately jump to images of empty wallets, unpaid bills, or children without food. But the sea has taught me otherwise.

Some of the most profound poverty I've witnessed wasn't in a slum or village—it was in the eyes of well-paid men on expensive ships. Not poverty of currency, but poverty of **connection**, **direction, love,** and **joy**.

Poverty could also be amidst Abundance.

One of the strangest paradoxes I've seen is this: **abundance outside, scarcity inside**.

A person can be Rich in terms of money. But if he lacked the emotional tools to connect, cope, or contribute, his heart hadn't been trained to sail through the storms of life.

Three Forms of Hidden Poverty at Sea (And on Shore)

Over time, I've come to identify **three hidden kinds of poverty**—ones we don't speak about enough:

1. Poverty of Relationships

Many seafarers live months, even years, in isolation. Some return home to find that their children have grown up without knowing them. Or their marriages have grown distant. I've seen officers with no one to call when we reached port.

No one to miss. No one to celebrate with. No one to cry for.

That's real poverty.

2. Poverty of Peace

You may be earning well, but you sleep poorly. Your mind races with anxiety, and your heart beats with worry. If your success comes at the cost of peace, is it truly success?

I once heard a junior officer say, "I'd give half my salary just to feel peace for one night." That struck me like lightning.

3. Poverty of Identity

Some men forget who they are beyond their rank or position. They cling to their job title because, without it, they feel like no one. But your true worth isn't in your position—it's in your **principles**, **actions**, and **how you treat others**.

Lessons from the Deck

The deck of a ship is like a classroom. It teaches by observation, not lecture.

Here's what it's shown me:

- The man who greets you with warmth daily, no matter his job, is rich.
- The man who hoards overtime but isolates himself is poor.
- The man who can listen with kindness is wealthy in humanity.
- The man who cannot express love, even to his children, is living in emotional debt.

Ask yourself:

- Do I give more than I take?
- Do I rest with ease at night?
- Do I know who I am when I'm not working?

Your answers will tell you where your richness—or poverty—lies.

Part 6: Life Doesn't Define You — You Define Life

There's a saying we often hear at sea: "You can't control the wind, but you can adjust the sails."

That's the essence of this section — you may not choose every wave life throws at you, but you get to decide how you sail through it.

The Voyage of Choice

I once sailed with a cadet named Arjun. He wasn't the strongest or the fastest, and he often struggled with tasks others found easy. But there was one thing about him that set him apart: he never gave up. When others complained, he quietly kept trying. When he failed, he asked for feedback.

I asked him, "Why do you keep trying when others have already judged you?"

He said, "Captain, I may not control how they see me, but I decide who I become."

That answer stayed with me. It reminded me that life doesn't define us — we define life through the choices we make.

The Helm is in Your Hands

Every ship has a helm — the wheel that steers her. No matter how wild the waters get, the helm remains your point of control. In life, your **mindset** is your helm.

It's not what happens to you, but **how you respond** that sets your direction.

I've seen men get demoted or suffer injury, yet rise again with courage. I've also seen people with promotions and privileges who still live in bitterness. What made the difference? One let life define them. The other took the helm back.

You are not the storm.

You are not the setback.

You are not the label someone once gave you.

You are the **captain** of your soul.

The Captain's Code for Defining Life

Let me give you some sea-tested truths — rules I've lived by, which have helped me steer my course even in the darkest waters:

- **Don't drift.** If you don't choose a direction, life will choose one for you.
- **Check your compass.** Regularly revisit your values, goals, and purpose.
- **Plot your course.** Break down your dreams into small, daily actions.
- **Avoid dead weight.** Let go of relationships and beliefs that no longer serve you.
- **Trust your crew.** Build a circle of people who lift you up, not pull you down.
- **Anchor when needed.** Sometimes, staying still is wiser than rushing forward.
- **Celebrate small harbors.** Every little win counts. A safe anchorage, a good meal, a call from a loved one — these are riches.

Who Is Writing Your Logbook?

On every ship, we maintain a logbook — a daily record of the ship's journey, condition, and events.

Now ask yourself: Who is writing the logbook of your life?

Is it your fear?

Is it someone else's expectations?

Is it society's definition of success?

Or is it **you, the captain**, pen in hand, writing each chapter deliberately?

The sea may be unpredictable. But your logbook is yours to write.

Part 7: The Cargo of Life

If life were a ship, then what we carry aboard — our *cargo* — defines the quality of our voyage.

Every ship has a cargo hold. It's filled carefully, item by item. It must be balanced, secured, and documented. If not, even the strongest ship can capsize once the weight is misplaced or not loaded as per the Stability Requirements.

The same is true in life.

What Are You Carrying?

Years ago, we were transiting through the Suez Canal on a container vessel. The load was uneven. A last-minute container loaded in haste had caused a slight list — a dangerous tilt of the vessel. It wasn't drastic, but enough for a trained captain to notice.

We couldn't proceed without adjusting the ballast water to rectify the tilt. We paused, rebalanced, and only then continued.

In life, many of us are sailing with a tilt — carrying mental or emotional cargo we never meant to load or never took time to rearrange.

Stress from unresolved relationships.

Habits that weigh down our health.

Old regrets and grudges, packed deep like hidden ballast.

Even success, if not understood well, can become a dead weight.

Your life becomes richer not just by adding more — but by knowing **what to carry**, **how to carry it**, and **what to let go**.

Toss the Dead Weight

Some ships are burdened with ballast — the water in the ship's tank used to keep the vessel stable. It has its uses, but too much of it slows you down.

Many people live with unnecessary ballast:

- Guilt they've carried for years.
- A job that doesn't inspire them anymore.
- Toxic relationships that anchor them in storms.

I recall a chief engineer who always seemed bitter, no matter how smooth the voyage. One day, over coffee, he shared a personal story — a business that failed long ago, and how he never forgave himself for it. He carried it like a cursed container, unopened but always present.

I told him, "Maybe it's time to throw that one overboard."

He laughed, but that moment stayed with him. Months later, he told me he had finally let it go. It didn't change his past, but it lightened his spirit.

Find out what you are still carrying that no longer serves your voyage.

Carry What Matters

Cargo is not always material. It can also be your **beliefs**, **skills**, and **values**.

To live a richer life, you must keep changing your internal cargo:

- Replace old fears with new learning.
- Replace comparison with gratitude.
- Replace complaints with curiosity.

Fill your hold with integrity, passion, learning, love, and discipline. Leave behind the fear, guilt, envy, and distraction.

You are not just a passenger in life. **You are the captain.** You choose what you carry. You decide what to offload.

Part 8: Anchors – What Keeps You Grounded

A ship is not always moving. Sometimes it must stop, stay in place, wait for orders, or wait for a storm to pass. But how does it stay steady in one spot despite wind, tide, or current?

We drop **anchor**.

In life, too, we need **anchors that keep us steady** when the world is shifting, and they **give us emotional depth and stability** as we move forward.

The Night We Lost Power

Let me begin with a memory.

One night, while approaching Osaka's berth, the vessel suddenly lost power. Lights flickered and died. The ship began to drift away — helpless, vulnerable, and at the mercy of the sea.

Immediately, I gave the order to drop anchor — not because we were near land, but because we needed to *hold the position* until the engineers could restore power. That anchor, heavy and silent, found its grip on the ocean floor. It didn't end the night. But it **kept us in place**, safe from being swept into dangerous waters.

That night, the anchor was our lifeline.

What Are Your Anchors in Life?

In life, when things fall apart — relationships fail, jobs end, illness strikes — **what keeps you from drifting?**

Your anchor may not be a physical object. It might be:

- Your **faith** or spiritual belief.
- **The unconditional love of your family.**
- A powerful **life purpose** you hold close.
- The **discipline** you've built over the years.

Anchors stop *you* from being swept away.

Sometimes when something happens to my loved ones while I am at sea, guilt washes over me for not being by their side. Regret hits me like a rogue wave. But I still had to lead. I am the captain. I had a crew depending on me.

What anchored me then was the values instilled in me by my father— duty, courage, and calmness. His teachings were my spiritual anchor. That didn't take away the grief, but they kept me steady.

Understanding Ballast: The Invisible Strength

While anchors hold a ship in place, **ballast** gives a moving ship stability. It's hidden — usually seawater placed in some tanks of the ship — but it plays a critical role.

Without ballast, a ship becomes top-heavy and unstable. Even small waves can tip it.

Similarly, in life, ballast is the **invisible weight** that helps you stay grounded while navigating challenges:

- Your **humility** that prevents arrogance.
- Your **inner discipline** that balances emotion.
- Your **core values** — honesty, perseverance, respect — that act as your keel.

Ballast doesn't slow you down. It gives you the strength to move **smoothly and safely**, even when the sea turns rough.

Do You Have Enough Ballast?

Ask yourself:

- When life shakes you, what keeps you from tipping over?
- Do you have **practices or rituals** that bring calm? (meditation, journaling, prayer, exercise?)
- Do you have **principles** you won't compromise on — even under pressure?
- Are you emotionally prepared for both calm and crisis?

Ballast isn't given to you. You must build it — one experience, one lesson, one reflection at a time.

And remember: Ballast is not meant to be baggage. While it's heavy, it *strengthens* you, not *burdens* you. But you need the right amount.

The Lesson for the Reader

There will be times when the engines of your life fail. Plans collapse. People leave. Dreams shatter.

When that happens, you will need something deeper than motivation. You'll need **something that holds you** — your anchor — and **something that strengthens you** — your ballast.

Trust in a few deep relationships, not a hundred shallow ones.

Conclusion: Charting the Course — Your Personal Voyage Begins

The journey doesn't truly begin until the course is set, the compass is checked, and the anchor is raised. You've just completed your first leg in *The Captain's Code* — and now, you hold the compass.

Before you go full ahead, ask yourself:

- Have I chosen a destination worth sailing toward?
- Am I ready for both calm seas and storms?
- Do I carry enough strength within — and support around — to keep going?

Because the voyage to a richer life isn't made by accident. It is **charted**, **navigated**, and **earned**.

You are not a passenger. **You are the Captain.**

Raise your anchor.

Set your sails.

The course to a **richer, deeper, fuller life** has begun.

CHAPTER 2

NAVIGATE BY THE STARS — ENJOY THE JOURNEY

"A sailor is not made just by the ship, but by how he reads the stars."

– Captain Utpal Haldar

Though a sailor has a compass, seafarers still look up — to the stars — ancient, reliable, and always present. The star gives them a position, to identify where the ship is located in a vast ocean.

Life, too, offers stars: inner strengths, personal talents, values, and passions that help you find your position, especially when everything around you is uncertain.

Here's how you can identify, cultivate, and apply those internal guiding lights as you journey toward a richer life.

Part 1: The Night Sky Is Never Empty — Finding Your Inner Constellation

I remember a particular night in the middle of the Atlantic Ocean. We were a thousand nautical miles from the nearest shore, cruising under a cloudless sky, the sea calm as polished glass. It was the midnight watch, and I had stepped out on the bridge wing for a breath of crisp, salty air.

What met my eyes was a sight only a sailor truly knows — the **entire night sky stretched wide open**, littered with stars, countless and eternal. No city lights, no noise, just a sacred silence punctuated by the rhythm of the waves and the **heavenly map above**.

At that moment, I felt so small, but also deeply connected. Out there, in the vast openness of the ocean, you begin to **sense your place in the universe**, not in terms of size, but in terms of meaning. And that's when a thought struck me like a well-timed wave: *even in the darkest night, the sky is never truly empty. The stars are always there — we just need to look up.*

Looking Inward to Look Up

Much like those stars, **your inner strengths—your** values, your talents, your passions—are always within you. But in the busyness of life, many forget to look up and take note of them.

At sea, when clouds cover the sky, we rely on instruments. But when technology fails, we fall back on the **old ways** — celestial navigation. We look for familiar constellations, like Orion, Cassiopeia, Scorpius, and Pegasus, and from them, we chart our position. Likewise, when life feels foggy and directionless, it's time to **find your personal constellations** — those traits and abilities that remind you of who you are and where you're going.

But here's the truth: many people avoid. If you can't navigate by stars, you don't know where you exist.

Discovering Your Polaris

Every captain knows the importance of Polaris, or the Pole Star, some call it the North Star. While the other stars seem to be apparently moving, Polaris stays fixed in the northern sky. It's reliable and consistent — the anchor of the all-stars.

In your life, your "Polaris" is your **core value or gift** — the thing that always brings you back to yourself, especially when everything else is drifting. For me, Polaris has always been a sense of **responsibility and purpose**. Whether managing a vessel with a multinational crew or making a difficult call in rough weather, I could always return to that guiding principle: *lead with integrity, and protect your people.*

What's your Polaris?

Maybe it's your empathy, your curiosity, your discipline, or your creativity. Maybe it's your ability to lift others' spirits. Or your commitment to learning, no matter what.

You won't find it in external noise. You'll find it in quiet moments — when you pause, reflect, and **listen to your own soul's compass**. Give yourself that quiet moment, alone, maybe on a lonely sea beach or in a garden at night with a clear, dark, starry sky. Just close your eyes and talk to yourself.

A Captain's Reflection

Let me share a quick story from my memory.

We had just departed from Kaohsiung on a container ship bound for Sydney. The sea was rough, and visibility was poor. On the second night, our GPS malfunctioned. I knew the vessel well and trusted my team, but the sudden reliance on manual position fixing brought back a wave of anxiety I hadn't felt in years.

I remember stepping out of the Navigation deck, which we call it bridge wing, that evening, my mind tangled with decisions. But as I looked up, the clouds parted just briefly — and there it was: the Big Dipper, pointing toward Polaris. A calming presence in a moment of uncertainty.

At that moment, all I needed was **clarity**– clarity of the ship's position. I thought of all the voyages I'd made, the crews I'd guided, the storms I'd weathered. And I remembered something a senior captain once told me as a young cadet: *"When you don't know what to do, do what aligns with your core."*

I returned to the bridge, took a deep breath, and calmly outlined our manual procedure to the officers. We sailed on safely.

That night reminded me that when you know your inner stars, you never sail blind.

Charting Your Inner Constellation

Each of us is made up of many stars, not just one. Your "constellation" is a collection of traits, passions, and experiences that form a pattern **unique to you**. The Greeks looked at the stars and saw hunters, lions, and serpents, and named them as Constellations. What do you see when you look inward?

Start small. It doesn't have to be big. Think about what you do effortlessly — what others often thank you for. What energizes you, even after a long day? These are clues. Maybe your inner constellation includes kindness, resilience, courage, or problem-solving.

Write them down. Talk to people who know you well. Revisit childhood joys. Often, the stars we lose sight of as adults are the ones we used to chase with open arms as children.

From Recognition to Cultivation

Of course, stars alone don't move a ship. Once you recognize your inner constellation, you must **nurture and apply** it.

Talents are like sails — useless unless hoisted.

Let's say you realize you're a natural communicator. Great — but are you using it? Are you building deeper relationships, mentoring others, or expressing yourself through writing or speaking?

Or perhaps your strength is discipline. Are you leading others by example? Are you using that structure to create meaningful progress in your personal goals?

Cultivate your inner strengths, take courses, read books, and nurture. Knowing your stars isn't enough. You must **sail by them**.

Lessons From the Night Sky

Here's what the stars have taught me over three decades at sea:
– **They are always present, even when hidden.**

- **They don't shout** — they shine silently.
- **They don't compare** — each has its place in the sky.
- **And most importantly, they guide best in the darkness.**

Right now, your life may have cloudy seasons, but the clarity you seek is already within you — if you look up and look in.

A Gentle Call to Action

This is your exercise. Tonight, after reading this chapter, before you sleep, step outside. Having a garden is great; if you have a terrace, it's also fine. Look at the sky – I insist. Even if you see no stars, close your eyes and imagine they are there.

As you close your eyes, what qualities shine in *your* sky?

Once you are back in your room, write them down. Reflect on how they've helped you navigate rough waters in the past.

Think of how you can use them more in the coming days — in your relationships, your work, your health, and your joy.

Because the stars of your life were not put there by accident. They are **your personal navigation system**, quietly waiting to guide you.

Trust them.

Trust yourself.

And sail on.

Part 2: Stars Don't Compete — They Simply Shine

There was a night in the South Pacific, somewhere between the Solomon Islands and Brisbane, that I still remember as clearly as if it happened yesterday. The sky was an endless dome of black velvet dusted with millions of stars. I stood alone on the bridge wing, the soft hum of the vessel beneath my boots, watching the sky in complete awe. Some stars blinked with brilliance, others faintly shimmered. They were not all equal in brightness or size, but each had its place. None tried to outshine the other. They simply… **shone**.

And then it hit me. These stars, so quietly magnificent, reminded me of something many people forget in their pursuit of success: **you don't need to compete to be valuable. You just need to shine in your own space.**

The Comparison Trap at Sea and in Life

Life ashore, much like life on a ship, often slips into comparison mode. We measure our worth by looking at someone else's logbook — their earnings, their titles, their appearance, their seemingly perfect voyage.

I've seen this even on vessels. A young third officer might look up to the chief officer and wonder if he'll ever be that respected. A newly promoted chief cook may compare herself to the previous one and feel she doesn't match up. But here's what I always tell my crew: *"The ship doesn't sail better when everyone tries to be the captain. It sails best when each person does their duty with heart."*

At sea, every role matters. The oiler, the bosun, the steward, the electrician — each one is a vital thread in the fabric of a safe voyage. If the motorman doesn't do his duty properly, it won't matter how sharp the navigator is. **Great voyages are built on harmony, not hierarchy.**

It's the same in life. You don't need to be someone else's version of successful. You just need to **be deeply aligned with your own light**.

The Silent Brilliance of Stars

One of the most beautiful things about stars is that they don't make noise. They don't shout, boast, or try to draw attention. They simply exist in quiet magnificence.

The most remarkable people I've met in my sailing life — from cadets to captains — were never the loudest in the room.

They were the ones who carried themselves with confidence born from self-knowledge. They didn't compare their path with others; they focused on their own journey, on improving each day.

Once, on a vessel headed to the Panama Canal, I met a wiper from the Philippines who barely spoke English. But every day, he showed up early, worked diligently, helped his mates, and smiled no matter the weather. One night, in a machinery emergency, he spotted a leaking gasket before anyone else. That small act prevented a major engine failure. He didn't compete. He just shone. And that made all the difference.

Lessons from the Celestial Chart

Ancient mariners didn't follow a single star. They used **constellations** and combinations of stars to form patterns. Each star played its part in helping the navigator to understand the position of the ship. None of the stars tried to dominate. They simply worked together in the sky's quiet choreography.

In life, imagine your community — your family, friends, colleagues — as a constellation. Each person has something valuable to contribute. **You don't have to burn brighter than someone else to matter. You just have to be true to your own light.**

Let others inspire you, but don't let them define you. Take guidance, not guilt. Admire the sparkle of others without dimming your own glow.

Finding Peace in Your Light

There's a quiet peace that comes when you stop comparing and start appreciating who you are. It's like sailing under calm skies, with the stars above and the sea gently rolling beneath. You realize that you are enough. That your journey is unfolding exactly as it should.

To know how to Shine Without Competing, please take a diary and write:

- **Acknowledge your strengths** — Make a list of what you do well. Not what others do better — what you uniquely offer.
- **Celebrate others** — Praise the success of others without feeling diminished. Their shine doesn't steal your light.
- **Focus on progress, not perfection** — Small daily growth adds up to greatness.
- **Be authentic** — Pretending to be someone else is exhausting. Being yourself is empowering.
- **Serve others** — When you shift from competing to contributing, your purpose deepens.

You Were Meant to Shine

Just as no two stars are alike, no two lives are the same. You weren't meant to follow someone else's chart. You were meant to chart your own course — with your own light.

Even when life feels heavy, uncertain, or slow, **keep showing up**. Keep giving your best. Keep believing that your presence matters.

Because it does.

Your life, like the stars above, is part of a grand design. You don't need to compete to be part of the sky.

You already are.

Part 3: The Sextant of Self-Discovery — Tools to Measure Your Growth

Every mariner remembers the first time they held a sextant. For me, it was a chilly morning somewhere off the coast of Italy. I was a cadet then — eager, nervous, and unsure of my place in the grand structure of the ship. My chief officer handed me the gleaming brass instrument with both hands and said, "This isn't just for stars and angles. It's a mirror. It'll show you where you are — and how far you've come."

At the time, I didn't fully understand. To me, the sextant was a mathematical puzzle — angles, declinations, time, calculations. But as the years passed and the oceans taught me their silent wisdom, I realized that **the sextant is more than a navigational tool. It's a metaphor for self-discovery and personal growth.**

In life, we all need our own version of a sextant — something that helps us measure where we are, reflect on where we've been, and recalibrate where we want to go.

The Sky as Your Guide — The Need for Reflection

At sea, a sextant works by measuring the angle between a celestial body (usually the sun, moon, planet, or star) and the horizon.

But before you can use it, you need two key conditions: a clear sky and a steady hand.

It's the same with life. To measure your growth — to truly understand who you are and who you're becoming — **you need clarity and stability**. That clarity comes from reflection. Stability comes from grounding routines, disciplines, values, and truth.

As a young officer, I used to think success was always upward — like climbing a mast. But there were nights when I stood alone on deck, scanning the sky for Polaris, when I began to understand: that **true progress isn't just forward movement. It's understanding your own coordinates — your inner position.**

Are you anchored in your values? Are you drifting from your dreams? Are you sailing with the current or fighting it?

These are the questions only a personal sextant can help answer.

Celestial Bodies and Inner Bearings — Choosing Your Markers

A sextant doesn't work without a known celestial reference — a fixed star, the sun, or a planet. You need something constant to measure against.

In life, what are your constants?

- **Is it your sense of purpose?**
- **Your family values?**
- **Your faith or inner compass?**
- **Your vision for the future?**

Calibration — The Importance of Honest Feedback

A sextant must be calibrated regularly. If it's misaligned, even by a small amount, your calculations could lead your position miles away. In life, we must also calibrate — through honest self-assessment and external feedback.

As a captain, I welcomed feedback from junior officers. It wasn't always easy, but it kept me sharp. Once, a young second officer quietly pointed out that my insistence on manual chart corrections after ECDIS (Electronic Chart Display and Information System) installation was slowing operations. I was reluctant at first. But his reasoning was sound. We conveyed the suggestion to the company to modify the operating procedure. I gained not just efficiency but respect from others.

Self-growth requires humility. Your personal sextant must be recalibrated through learning, listening, and adjusting.

Keep a diary. Ask yourself regularly and write:

- Am I reacting or responding?
- Am I listening or waiting to speak?
- Am I growing bitter or better?

These questions will help you adjust your internal course.

Journaling: A Modern Sextant for the Soul

One of the best personal practices you should adopt is journaling. After every few days or occasions, spend a few days writing down lessons, reflections, moments of pride, and scope for growth. It's your modern sextant — a log of your personal ocean.

You don't need to be a writer. Just be honest. Write about what challenged you, what made you feel alive, what drained your spirit, and what filled your sails – No long stories, just basic points, and highlights.

Over time, patterns will emerge. You'll begin to **see the map of your growth** — and navigate life with more intention.

Read Your Position Often

Just as a captain wouldn't dare sail days without checking position, you must not go too long without **checking in with yourself**. Ask:

- What am I learning?
- What am I avoiding?
- What am I becoming?

A sextant doesn't lie. And neither does the quiet voice inside you — if you listen.

So, look to your own horizon. Choose your stars — your values, your goals, your purpose. Hold your inner sextant steady. Take honest readings often. Calibrate when necessary.

And remember, growth is not about reaching port quickly. It's about knowing you're heading in the right direction — no matter the weather.

Part 4: Celestial Navigation — When Position Is Calculated Based on Stars

It was midnight in the South Pacific, and the sky above the bridge was a blanket of velvet pierced by a thousand brilliant stars. The sea was calm — unusually so — with the ship gliding like a ghost across the mirrored surface. I stepped out onto the bridge wing with my sextant in hand, the brass cool against my palm, and lifted it toward the heavens.

This was my favorite time of day — the *midnight watch.* Most of the world was asleep, but for us at sea, the stars were awake, whispering age-old secrets of direction and destiny.

I was calculating our position using celestial navigation — a skill that might seem outdated in the era of GPS and electronic charts, but to a mariner, it's a rite of passage. It's also a powerful metaphor for life: **when the world around you offers no clear road signs, you look to the stars — to something higher and eternal — to understand where you are.**

Lost Without Satellites — A Crisis at Sea

There was a time, many years ago, when this metaphor became reality.

We were in the North Pacific Ocean when our GPS failed. A software glitch — coupled with a backup system that refused to cooperate — left us temporarily blind. Our ECDIS (Electronic Chart Display and Information System) was giving warning alarms echoing in the wheelhouse like a heartbeat gone wrong.

I called the second officer and said, "Let's do it the old way. Break out the sextant."

We took sun sights that day, and star sights that night. Using three celestial bodies — Sirius, Altair, and Antares — we plotted our position. The process took longer, sure. But it worked. We knew exactly where we were.

That unexpected pause gave us time to teach the cadets celestial navigation, a skill they might never have otherwise learned in our GPS-dependent world. It was a moment of pride for the entire team. Not just because we solved a problem, but because we reconnected with the timeless wisdom of sailors before us. Long before satellites beamed coordinates into our palms, the stars had guided humanity across vast oceans.

And they still can.

Life Without GPS — When Your Path Feels Lost

Sometimes in life, we lose our own GPS. Plans fall apart. Career stall. Relationships end. We feel adrift. The question arises: *Where am I? How did I get here?*

That's when you must turn to your inner stars — the constants that have always been with you, even if you haven't noticed.

For some, it's faith. For others, it's the memory of a parent's guidance, a teacher's voice, or a childhood dream. These are your celestial bodies — always above, always shining, even on cloudy nights.

In those dark moments, you can still calculate your position—not with a satellite, but with reflection, values, and inner truth.

Three-Point Fix — Plotting Your Inner Location

In celestial navigation, the most accurate way to determine position is to take sightings from three different stars. Each gives a position line, and where those three lines intersect is where you are.

In life, you can take a "three-star fix" too. Here's how I do it:

1. **The Star of Purpose** – Why do I do what I do? Am I still aligned with my deeper purpose?
2. **The Star of People** – Who are the most meaningful people in my life? Am I investing in those relationships?
3. **The Star of Peace** – Am I at peace with the person I am becoming?

When you reflect on these three, you can triangulate your current position — emotionally, spiritually, and personally. And from there, you can navigate forward with clarity.

Cloudy Skies

Of course, there are days when the sky is overcast. No stars, no moon. Just shades of grey.

This happens in life, too — moments of grief, confusion, or burnout. You can't see your stars. But here's the truth sailors know well: **just because the stars are hidden doesn't mean they're gone.**

In such times, you sail on dead reckoning — using your past position, compass, and known direction to estimate your current approximate position. You trust your training, your instincts, and your experience.

Likewise, in life, when clarity vanishes, fall back on what you know:

- Your values.
- Your discipline.
- Your track record.

They'll carry you through the fog until the stars reappear.

Part 5: The Joy of the Voyage — Not Just the Destination

The Port Wasn't the Point

I still remember our voyage from Tokyo to the Panama Canal when I was a Second Officer. We had a full container load, the crew was well-trained, and I was excited about the smoothness of the upcoming sail. Everything was in order. The weather forecasts were fair, and we had nearly a month of open sea ahead.

Now, one might assume that the highlight of this journey was the arrival—the thrill of seeing the Panama Canal and Port of Manzanillo come into view, the paperwork complete, and the ship safely berthed.

But it wasn't.

Looking back, what stays with me isn't the arrival. It's the laughter over meals with the crew, the dolphins that danced alongside the bow wave in the mid-Pacific, the captivating flying fish, the night watches under a full moon, the unknown ocean organisms that illuminate the waves in a dark night, and the stories shared on the bridge at midnight.

That voyage taught me something that no chart or compass could reveal:

The journey itself is the treasure—not just the port where it ends.

The Destination Delusion

We're conditioned, almost from childhood, to think in terms of destinations:

- "I'll be happy when I become a captain."
- "I'll feel successful once I earn this much."
- "I'll relax when I retire."

Life becomes a checklist. Port after port. Promotion after promotion. But what if you reach your destination only to discover it wasn't what you expected? Or worse—what if you miss the beauty of the voyage because your eyes are always glued to the horizon?

At sea, we quickly learn that voyages rarely go exactly as planned. Currents shift. Storms arrive uninvited. Machinery fails. But the skilled mariner doesn't curse the waves—he adjusts the sails, studies the skies, and finds meaning in the process.

So it is with life.

The Captain's Reflection — A Story from the Bridge

Years later, during a monsoon voyage in the Indian Ocean, I stood alone on the bridge, sipping my coffee while the ship swayed under grey skies. It was one of those introspective moments.

I had crossed oceans. Trained dozens of officers. Saved lives. Delivered millions of dollars' worth of cargo.

And yet, at that moment, I wasn't thinking about my achievements. I was thinking about the journey that brought me here—the countless miles, the mistakes I learned from, the small kindnesses I received from strangers in ports far from home.

I thought of a cook from India, who once gave up his phone call so a cadet could speak to his sick mother. I thought of the bosun who, during rough seas, tied down every loose container on deck without being asked.

None of these moments showed up on a résumé. But **they were on a voyage.** They shaped the man I became.

Charting Life: The Perils of Linear Thinking

In life, we often treat goals like ports:

- "Graduate college."
- "Get married."
- "Buy a house."
- "Start a business."
- "Retire comfortably."

But ships aren't made to remain in port. They're built to sail.

A life obsessed with destinations becomes a straight, rigid line—full of pressure, comparison, and burnout. But when you fall in love with the **process**—the daily effort, the quiet sunrises, the teamwork, the setbacks, the learning—that's when life becomes *alive*.

I often tell young cadets, "Yes, aim for the Captain's chair. But don't miss the joy of being a third Officer. These days won't come again."

When Storms Delay the Arrival

A few years ago, we were nearing Hokkaido, Japan, when a tropical storm forced us to hold position offshore for three days. We were taking shelter near the Kuril Islands. The crew was restless. Some were anxious about missed shore leave. Others just wanted to dock and go home.

However, I used that time to teach safety lessons to the junior officers. We discussed maritime case studies, real-life failures, and how to deal with pressure. It became one of the most engaging moments of mentorship in my career.

The lesson?

The storm delayed the destination—but it deepened the journey.

Reflections for Shore and Sea

Whether you're navigating a sea or a career, whether you're commanding a ship or running a family, the same truth applies:

- **Your value isn't just in what you reach.**
- **It's in how you live while you journey.**

Ask yourself:

- Am I fully present in the current chapter of my life?
- Am I enjoying the voyage, or am I too focused on the next port?
- What memories am I creating today?

Lessons for a Richer Life

Let's chart this out like a passage plan:

- **Waypoint 1: Embrace Delays**
- Delays can be detours to growth. What feels like a setback often becomes your greatest teacher.
- **Waypoint 2: Celebrate Small Wins**
- Every safe watch, every helpful hand, every laugh shared—they're worth anchoring in memory.
- **Waypoint 3: Be Present on Deck**
- Don't miss the sea around you because your eyes are fixed on the lighthouse ahead.
- **Waypoint 4: Savor the Sail**
- Life, like the sea, is in motion. Your greatest stories will come from the sail—not the port.

Final Reflection — Sail by Your Own Stars

You've just navigated one of the most sacred truths of the sea — and of life: *The stars above are only useful if you choose to look up.*

In this chapter, we've stepped out onto the bridge, into the silence of the night, and learned how to find our inner constellation — the traits, values, and passions that quietly illuminate our true path. The journey is not about rushing to the next port — it's about learning to read the sky above and the soul within.

So here is your call to action:

- Look within. What qualities define your inner sky?
- Find your Polaris. What truth always brings you back to yourself?
- Stop competing. Stars don't. They simply shine.
- Use your sextant. Reflect, recalibrate, and rediscover your direction.
- *Most of all — enjoy the journey.*

Because your voyage is not defined by how fast you reach your goals, but by how deeply you live along the way. The laughter, the detours, the quiet wins — they are the voyage.

The stars are waiting.

Now step outside, look up — and sail by your own light.

You are not lost. You are discovering. Keep going.

Captain's Verse — Sail by Starlight

You were not born to drift ashore,
Nor follow maps drawn long before.
You carry stars inside your chest,
A compass beating in your breast.
When clouds roll in and paths are blind,
Look not ahead, but deep inside.
The voyage true is not the end—
But how you live, what light you send.
So sail by stars, not by the crowd,
And make your silence brave and loud.
You are the captain. You must steer—
The stars you need are always near.

CHAPTER 3

READ THE WIND, ADJUST THE SAILS – THE ART OF ADAPTABILITY

"We can't direct the wind, but we can adjust our sails."

Part 1: The Wind Doesn't Ask Permission — Change is Constant

There's a quiet kind of arrogance that creeps into a sailor's heart when the sea is calm and the sky shines blue.

We had just left Vancouver, Canada, bound for Tokyo. It was early summer, and everything about the voyage looked perfect on paper. The Pacific stretched out like shining glass, the wind gentle, our vessel—a massive container ship—gliding forward with the grace of a dancer. We were at full speed, covering more than 500 nautical miles a day. The crew was relaxed. The coffee flowed freely, and laughter echoed in the alleyways.

But life at sea, much like life itself, has a way of turning in a heartbeat.

I still remember the weather report that came through late in the afternoon. A low-pressure system was forming fast over the Gulf of Alaska. At first glance, it seemed distant, something we could simply dodge. With a ship of our speed and size, it wasn't an unreasonable assumption because we have the ability to run away 500 nautical miles in one day. We plotted a new route to skirt its projected path. The goal was simple: stay clear, stay safe.

What we didn't know was that the storm had no intention of keeping its word.

The Shift

Midnight brought a different truth. The wind rose—subtle at first, like a whisper against the steel hull. Then, like an uninvited guest kicking down the door, it howled. New weather updates rolled in. The storm had shifted course—and intensified. What was supposed to be a glancing threat had now become a head-on confrontation.

There's no pause button at sea. You can't pull over and wait it out. You deal with what's coming, ready or not.

"Start the heavy weather preparation," I instructed.

The crew moved like clockwork. We initiated the checklist—each task vital, each step crucial. Cargo lashing was double-checked. Engine room secured. Loose equipment is tied down. Stability double-checked. We knew the drill, but drills are like dancing in rehearsal. Reality doesn't always stick to choreography.

When the Sky Falls

The first wave that slapped our starboard side didn't feel like water—it felt like a living wall. The vessel began to roll and pitch violently. Some chairs that were tied, ripped open, and tumbled. Some dining plates and glasses broke and started sliding off the mess room floor, and the once-calm corridors turned into obstacle courses. Within hours, several of the crew were seasick, gripping onto railings or curled in their bunks. Others—my warriors—stood firm with me on the bridge and in the Engine room.

We fought back—not with fists, but with preparation, emergency actions, courage, and instinct sharpened over the years.

Down in the engine room, the heart of our ship, the engineers were fighting their own battle. The main engine tripped several times as sensors breached safety limits. Restarting it wasn't just a matter of flipping a switch. It meant climbing steep stairs up and down a few floors, as the ship kept on tilting side to side at terrifying angles, maneuvering through heat and noise, and danger. I could hear them on the radio—short, urgent exchanges. No panic, just purpose.

We were a crew tested by the sea, and each moment in that storm asked a question: Will you adapt, or will you break?

When the Wind Wins — And Still You Sail

Twelve hours passed like twelve lifetimes. The storm gave us no mercy. But neither did we ask for it. We held our course. We didn't surrender.

Finally, in the late morning, the sky began to lighten. The waves, once monstrous, started to tame. The wind, having spent its rage, began to retreat into silence. It didn't feel like a victory—it felt like survival.

As the sea calmed and the sun pierced the thinning clouds, I stood on the bridge, damp with sweat, a bit tired, eyes burning with exhaustion—and pride.

Yes, we had made it.

But it wasn't just the ship that had sailed through. It was each one of us—tested, rattled, but stronger.

Lessons from the Storm

That voyage taught me more about adaptability than any classroom or seminar ever could. Here's the truth: **life, like the**

ocean, changes without asking permission. It doesn't consult your plans. It doesn't care about your comfort zone. It shifts, it storms, it surprises.

But here's the magic—if you're willing to adjust your sails, you don't just survive the storm… You grow from it.

So, what does that mean for the sea?

Maybe your "storm" isn't in the Pacific. Maybe it's a sudden layoff, a heartbreak, a medical diagnosis, or a failed business. You thought life was going one way, and then it didn't. The weather changed. The course was altered.

And this is where adaptability enters—not as a weakness, but as a strength.

Adaptability Is an Attitude

To be adaptable isn't just to react. It's to read the signs early, to stay alert, and to adjust quickly. It means holding on to your **purpose** but being flexible with your **plans**. It means you prepare for what you can, but you're also mentally ready for the unknown.

Think about this: we couldn't stop the storm, but we could prepare for it. We couldn't hold the waves back, but we could reinforce the cargo lashings. We couldn't stop the engine from tripping, but we could restart it every time.

Life is no different.

You can't always stop what's coming, but you can control how you show up.

You Don't Have to Be Unshakable—Just Willing

People often confuse adaptability with weakness. But in reality, it takes immense strength to bend when others break. Trees that survive hurricanes aren't the stiff ones—they're the ones that sway with the wind and snap back afterward.

There's a quote I love: "It's not the strongest of the species that survives, nor the most intelligent, but the one most responsive to change."

In your own life, adaptability might look like:

- Starting over when things fall apart
- Asking for help when you thought you could do it alone
- Learning new skills when your old ones become obsolete
- Letting go of something—even someone—that no longer aligns with your journey

The wind will shift. That's a promise. Your job is to shift with it, not against it.

Final Reflection: Embrace the Unexpected

You may not be sailing a 200,000-ton container ship, but you're captaining something just as precious—**your life**.

And just like the sea, life won't ask before it changes course.

It will throw headwinds, cross currents, and unexpected gales. You will be tested—perhaps not by rolling waves, but by layoffs, grief, rejection, or doubt.

Your strength won't come from controlling the weather.

It will come from adjusting your sails.

From trusting your crew—your friends, your family.

From relying on your tools—your discipline, your faith, your resilience.

From learning, not just surviving.

Because in the end, life isn't about avoiding storms.

It's about becoming the kind of person who sails through them—and comes out wiser, smarter on the other side.

Part 2: Trim the Sails — Small Adjustments, Big Impact

The open sea teaches us many things, but perhaps none so subtle and powerful as the art of trimming the sails.

Navigating with Precision

On a ship, every degree of course, every knot of speed, every shift in weight distribution matters. If you're even a fraction off, a small mistake at sea can magnify into a big problem hundreds of nautical miles later.

This isn't just about steering a ship—it's a metaphor for life. The idea that we need massive overhauls to change our course is misleading. Often, it's not the big decisions but the tiny, conscious tweaks that make the difference between sinking and sailing forward in life.

Are you stressed out because of your workload? A small change like going to bed 30 minutes earlier or taking 10 minutes to journal your thoughts each morning can change your entire mental landscape.

Is your relationship struggling? It doesn't always take a grand romantic gesture. A five-minute heartfelt conversation each evening can shift the entire emotional climate between two people. Give time. Make small adjustments.

Are your finances always strained? You might not need a raise—you might just need to track your expenses more closely for a month. That alone might reveal small leaks draining your financial hull.

These are your sails—your levers of control. Trim them.

The Rudder of Relationships

I've seen more damage done to relationships from neglect than from open conflict. Like a ship slightly off course, most relationships don't explode—they drift apart. All they need is a slight correction.

At sea, even a 1-degree error can send you hundreds of miles off your intended destination if unchecked. Likewise, a partner who feels unheard for weeks, a child who's rarely hugged, a friend you've stopped calling—they drift. One day, you wake up and wonder how you grew so far apart.

But just as easily, you can steer back.

A message of appreciation. A walk after dinner. A quiet conversation with no agenda. A cup of tea with a friend. These are not grand gestures, but they are sail-trimming moments. They align your course and bring you back toward the ones who matter most.

As a captain, I kept a practice of checking on my crew individually—not for daily reports, but for genuine well-being. It may have taken ten minutes of my day, but built years of loyalty. The same principle applies at home.

Financial Bearings — Tiny Turns Toward Abundance

When you steer a ship, you learn to read currents and tides. Some will carry you, others will resist you. Knowing when to adjust is the key.

Finances are similar. Most people don't go broke from one large purchase—they bleed from dozens of unnoticed leaks. A streaming service here, an unused subscription there, daily impulse buys that add up like barnacles on a hull.

Trimming the financial sails isn't about cutting joy from your life. It's about smart alignment. Small savings invested wisely can become wealth over time. Tracking your spending for even a week is like checking your ship's course—it tells you where you're truly headed.

At sea, fuel is one of our biggest costs. Small changes—reducing speed during calm weather, choosing favorable currents, or running generators efficiently—make a huge difference to the company.

In life, your financial habits are a reflection of your values and discipline. Master them through small, consistent corrections.

The Course Ahead — Daily Course Corrections

Imagine setting sail without ever checking your heading again. Ridiculous, right? Yet many of us set life goals—get healthier, be happier, save more—and never stop to check our progress.

Every good navigator does regular course corrections. They check the compass, verify their position, and adjust. Life is the same.

A five-minute morning routine to set your intention. A weekly review of your goals. A monthly check-in on your emotional state.

It's not about obsessing. It's about awareness.

When I mentor young officers, I tell them, "Never trust automation too long. Check hand steering, check your heading, check your position. The ocean is alive, and drift is real."

So is life. Trim your sails regularly.

In relationships, health, wealth, and purpose, don't wait for a crisis to turn the wheel. The small decisions you make today—right now—will determine where you arrive tomorrow.

A ship trimmed well can glide even in heavy weather. A life trimmed well can find calm amidst the chaos.

Part 3: Reef the Sails Before the Storm — Anticipate and Prepare

There's an old sailor's saying: *"Reef early, and you'll rarely regret it."* It means that a smart mariner doesn't wait until the wind is howling and the sails are tearing to act. He reads the signs—the sudden hush before the wind picks up, the subtle shift in the clouds, the low, steady fall in barometric pressure—and makes his preparations before the storm arrives.

In life, just like at sea, the ones who thrive are not always the fastest or the strongest, but the ones who are *prepared.*

The Warning Signs

I was sailing from Tokyo to Hong Kong on a large container vessel. The voyage was routine, with smooth seas and a light breeze playing over the deck. It was early in the typhoon season, but we kept a close eye on the weather updates, as every captain should.

One evening, as I was standing with my chief officer over a cup of coffee in the chart room, a new weather report came in. A typhoon had formed far to the east of Taiwan. It seemed a little far. We were still days away from entering her potential path. But the next day barometer had started to dip subtly. The cloud cover seemed different that evening—thicker, with a strange stillness in the air. I felt it in my bones, that quiet tension a sailor learns to respect.

Some might have dismissed it. After all, the skies were still clear. But instinct, backed by experience, told me this was not a time for complacency. We decided to act *early*.

Rerouting and Reinforcing

Together with my navigation team, we plotted an alternate course. It would take us slightly longer to reach Hong Kong, but it would steer us along the outer fringes of the typhoon's projected path. Meanwhile, all crew was briefed. We initiated heavy weather preparations. All loose equipment was secured. Lashing on every container stack was double-checked. Critical systems were inspected. We didn't cut corners.

Checklists were ticked off, one by one. We held safety meetings and reviewed our emergency response protocols. We weren't panicking—we were simply *preparing*.

As expected, within 36 hours, the typhoon almost followed the predicted path and moved faster than originally predicted. Had we waited even half a day longer to act, we would have been caught far closer to its center, and the consequences could have been severe.

Instead, by the time we encountered the outer fringes, we experienced only a mild swell and moderate winds. No cargo was lost. No equipment was damaged. Not a single crew member was injured.

We sailed on, calm in our quiet triumph.

Lessons from the Storm You Don't Face

Here's the thing: no one saw the hours of preparation we did before the weather turned. No one applauded the calm voyage or the fact that we avoided chaos. **That's the paradox of preparation—*when it works, it looks like nothing happened.***

But that's the point. True mastery is when you steer around trouble, not through it.

In life, storms come in all forms—a job loss, a health scare, a relationship crisis, or financial strain. Most of them arrive with a warning, either subtle or loud. They send ripples before they hit. A doctor's raised eyebrow during a routine checkup. A growing tension in your marriage. That uneasiness when you swipe your card, unsure if it will clear.

The mistake most people make is *waiting*—waiting until the blood test confirms the issue, waiting until the fight becomes a breakup, waiting until the debt is too big to manage. Waiting, instead of watching and preparing.

A wise sailor reads the sky. A wise person reads life's signals.

Anticipation as a Life Skill

Anticipation isn't anxiety—it's awareness.

There's a difference between living in fear and living with foresight. Fear paralyses. Foresight empowers.

When I mentor junior officers, I often tell them, "You don't prepare because the weather *might* be bad. You prepare because it *can* be. It's the discipline of readiness that defines a good officer from a lucky one." **You cannot be lucky every time.**

After this chapter, I insist that you take a moment, dim the lights, close your eyes when everything is calm around you, and ask yourself:

- What storms might be forming on your horizon?
- Is your health quietly calling for attention? When did you check your health last?
- Are your finances beginning to wobble?
- Is someone you love drifting away, even just a little?

Open your eyes, take a notebook, and jot it down. You don't need to panic if you get a negative answer. You don't need to overhaul everything. But maybe it's time to reef the sails—tighten things up, adjust course slightly, and check your systems.

Reefing in Real Life

Reefing the sails in advance isn't flashy. It's not dramatic. But it's powerful.

In your relationships, it means having that difficult conversation *before* resentment sets in.

In your health, it means scheduling that check-up *before* the symptoms escalate.

In your work, it means upskilling, networking, or building a cushion *before* the economy turns – constantly upgrade yourself.

In your finances, it means saving while things are good so you're not desperate when they're not.

It's all about preparing in the calm, so you don't fall apart in the storm.

Some of the most valuable work you'll ever do will be invisible to the world.

But like the unseen preparations that keep a ship safe during a typhoon, those quiet acts of readiness are what carry you through life's rough waters.

Don't wait for the wind to howl before you act. Don't let the storm catch you by surprise. Be the one who sees the signs, makes the moves, and keeps the ship steady—because you were wise enough to reef the sails before the storm.

Part 4: When the Wind Shifts — Pivot With Grace

At sea, you learn one lesson very early: the wind has no loyalty to your plan. It changes direction without warning, and if you fight it, you're likely to stall—or worse, drift into danger. But if you adjust your sails and pivot with grace, the same wind that threatened your journey can carry you to a safer, even better destination.

Life is no different.

We often set out with a fixed course—an idea of who we want to be, where we want to go, and how fast we should get there. But what happens when conditions change? When pirates prowl your path, when storms block your way, when your inner compass starts to feel off?

Let me tell you a story—one where we had to make such a pivot.

A Voyage Rerouted: The Pirate Waters of the Arabian Sea

At that time, I was a young officer. We were sailing from Singapore to the Suez Canal, passing through the Arabian Sea—a region that, at the time, had grown increasingly dangerous due to piracy. Our cargo was high-value, and the vessel was large and vulnerable if caught unaware.

Before departure, we were well informed. Intelligence reports warned of a few hijackings in the area near the Gulf of Aden. Despite that, the fastest and most economical route remained the one that cut close to Somalia's coast—right through known pirate waters.

There was tension in the air even as we departed Singapore. We held additional security briefings. Razor wires were installed along the perimeter of the deck. Extra lookouts were assigned. Fire hoses were pressurized and ready. And yet, deep inside, I knew that sometimes, preparedness isn't enough—adaptability is essential.

A Threat Emerges

Two days into the high-risk area, during my watch in the afternoon, we picked up a radar contact about 12 nautical miles behind our vessel. A fast-moving skiff—a red flag. We adjusted the course slightly to assess, hoping it was just a fishing boat. I alerted the Captain and then the crew.

Then came the second skiff, from another direction. Both began to close in.

My instincts screamed.

The captain decided on an emergency maneuver. Our original route, optimized for speed and fuel economy, was abandoned in an instant. The captain ordered a hard starboard, farther north, but safer. It would cause delays to our arrival, burn more fuel, and alter all planned schedules. But that didn't matter at that moment. We were heading into the wind, which was blowing hard, creating waves. We headed into the wind at full speed. The small boat could not face the strong wind and started pitching and pounding heavily while chasing the ship. The pirate boat turned back and left us. The mission had changed: from delivery to survival.

Leading Through the Pivot

At that moment, the challenge was not by how tightly I could stick to the plan, but how swiftly we could let go of it.

Later, we gathered the crew and explained the situation honestly: "We may be taking a longer route, but we'll be taking a safer one. We'd rather arrive late than never."

There were no complaints. The crew felt the tension too. They were relieved to see their captain value lives over timetables and safety over pride.

In the end, the skiffs never reached us. Perhaps our maneuvers and strategies were enough. Perhaps luck played a part. But I believe it was the decision to pivot that saved us.

The Grace in Changing Course

We often treat change as something shameful—as if abandoning the original plan means we've failed. But the truth is, it takes more courage to change direction than to stubbornly stick to the new course.

Think about your own life.

Have you ever pursued a career path because it was "expected," only to find it didn't fulfill you?

Have you ever stayed in a relationship with your partner or a friend long past its healthy stage because you didn't want to admit it had changed?

Have you ignored signs of burnout because changing direction felt like giving up?

Here's the truth: Pivoting isn't quitting. It's evolving. The best sailors don't fight the wind—they work with it. They adjust their sails, reroute their voyage, and continue moving forward—even if they end up taking a longer route.

When Plans Break, Clarity Can Emerge

Sometimes, it's only when the original plan is disrupted that we discover what truly matters.

The detours often teach you more than the destinations.

A lost job can lead to a new passion.

A breakup can lead to self-discovery.

A failed venture can lead to a wiser, stronger comeback.

Not how tightly we cling to our plans, but how gracefully we let them go when the moment calls for it – that is what matters.

So, when your own life brings unexpected winds—when the job changes, the relationship shifts, or the road ahead disappears—remember this:

You are the captain of your own voyage.

And sometimes, the bravest thing you can do… is turn the wheel.

Part 5: Adaptation Builds Strength

There's one particular voyage I'll never forget. It not only tested my ship and crew but also revealed the true character of those onboard and the kind of inner strength that only adversity can summon.

The Calm Before the Tempest

We had departed from Busan, South Korea, bound for Long Beach, California, with a full load of containers and a well-rehearsed crew. For the first few days, the voyage was uneventful. The sea was friendly, the sky mostly clear, and the ship hummed along the Pacific route as if she were enjoying the calm too.

Then came the warning.

A tropical storm forming near Guam was predicted to intensify and move across our planned route. At first, the forecast showed it might veer north—but we knew there was no point gambling with tropical systems. The crew gathered in the conference room, weather charts open, eyes scanning the pressure lines and wind patterns.

We made the call: alter course southward, increase surveillance, and prepare for heavy weather. We adjusted ballast, checked lashings, inspected watertight doors, and ticked every box on the heavy weather checklist. The crew moved with urgency, but no panic. This was routine—until it wasn't.

Chaos Unleashed

That night, the sea turned against us. The wind came howling—first a whisper, then a shriek. Waves towered like mountains, slamming against the bow, sending excessive sprays over the bridge windows. Visibility dropped to near zero. The radar lit up like a war zone, yellow patches swirling and overlapping.

Then the engine alarms started.

Our main engine was struggling—pitching and rolling were pushing the engine parameters out of tolerance. The engineers worked around the clock, drenched in sweat, making manual adjustments in the control room and climbing ladders in a violently swaying engine room. I could see exhaustion in their eyes, but also a spark of fire. No one complained.

One of our deck officers, new to the vessel and still finding his sea legs, looked at me and said, "Captain, I didn't sign up for this."

I smiled, "My boy, you didn't sign up for calm waters either."

We adjusted the course again, tightening our path to skim the edge of the storm. It meant longer hours, more fuel, and increased watch-standing—but it was the right call. Slowly, after nearly 18 hours of battering, the wind began to ease. The sea, though still heaving, started to breathe more calmly.

When the sun rose the next day, a pale orange glow behind clouds, the ship was still afloat, its cargo secured, and its crew intact. We had made it.

The Lessons That Salt Teaches

Storms at sea are great metaphors for life's trials. There are days when everything goes wrong—when your plans fail, your emotions spiral, your relationships fray. That's when your adaptability becomes your anchor.

At sea, we adapt not just out of preference but out of necessity. A rigid mindset sinks ships. It's the same in life. Relationships evolve, careers pivot, health changes—**either you learn to shift your sails, or you find yourself adrift.**

During that voyage, I saw the power of preparation, yes, but more importantly, I witnessed the strength of adaptation: the engineers improvising solutions to procedures when systems didn't work as expected, the deck crew re-lashing cargo in high wind gusts that could knock a man overboard, the junior officer regaining his courage through action. Adaptation isn't a single act—it's a mindset.

What the Storm Leaves Behind

Storms no longer frighten—they educate. They remind me of who I am, what I'm capable of, and how essential adaptability is—not just to sail a ship, but to live a meaningful life.

Each wave we ride over, each gust we push through, teaches us a little more about endurance, humility, and grace under pressure. And when the storm finally passes, we emerge changed—not broken, but seasoned.

To the reader navigating your own tempest: don't fear the storm. Prepare for it, adapt to it, and trust that when the winds settle, you'll find yourself not only afloat—but stronger than ever before.

Every storm leaves a trace.

After this chapter, I insist you close your eyes, stay calm, and think of your life. What storm have you faced recently?

- Was it a health scare?
- A failing business?
- Is a relationship falling apart?
- Or perhaps a time you were simply overwhelmed and directionless?

Note the points down. Now ask yourself: How did you adapt? What did that moment teach you? Who stood beside you, and who fell away?

Your life is supported by people who rise to the occasion—or not. And like a good sailor, you must remember to:

- Read the signs early
- Prepare before the storm hits
- Rely on your training, not just emotion
- **And most importantly—trust that every storm passes away**

Some of the strongest bonds you'll ever form—whether at sea or in life—will be forged in rough weather.

When the skies finally clear and the ship steadies on her course again, take a breath. And know that you are not the same person who entered the storm.

You are more.

Captain's Life Lesson:

"Don't curse the storm. Sail through it, adapt with it, and let it reveal the sailor within you."

Part 6: The Rudder and the Will — You Still Steer Your Ship

The Rudder Represents Your Will

In navigation, a rudder is a small yet powerful control surface. It doesn't stop the wind, nor can it flatten waves. But with it, the ship can change direction, stabilize, and keep going — even in chaos.

In life, your will is your rudder.

You may be hit by job loss, illness, heartbreak, or failure — storms of life. But the ability to decide how you will respond? That is still in your hands.

Just like at sea, when the wind changes or storms arise, **you *don't* throw your hands up and let the ship drift**. You grip the helm tightly. You think calmly. You steer intentionally.

The sea has taught me this lesson over and over: Adaptability doesn't mean helplessness. It means adjusting your sails, but always steering your own ship.

Rudder Moments in Daily Life

You don't have to be a captain on the high seas to apply this.

You can't control the wave. But you can **steer your ship**.

Here's how you use your rudder:

- **Pause** — Don't react immediately. Hold steady.
- **Assess** — Gather your bearings. What are the facts?
- **Decide** — Where do you want to go from here?
- **Act** — Turn the helm with intention. Make small adjustments and change direction.
- **Believe** — Trust in your ability to navigate, even when visibility is low.

– You may not see the shore yet. But with your hand on the wheel, you're heading for it no longer drifting.

Why the Rudder Matters More Than the Wind

The wind will always blow. Sometimes in your favor. Sometimes directly against you. But the rudder remains constant.

It's the tool of choice, a tool for adaptability, to divert, to navigate – where you wish to go.

If you let go of the helm, the sea will decide your course. But if you hold on — calmly, firmly — you decide.

That's not just seafaring wisdom. That's life.

In the end, it's not about how strong the wind is — it's about whether you've got the will to hold the wheel.

And trust me, Captain — **you do**.

"Adaptability is the Sailor's Art — Knowing When to Yield, When to Shift, and When to Stand Firm"

There's an old truth that every seasoned sailor carries deep in their bones, which I repeat: "**You can't control the wind, but you can always adjust your sails**". It's not just a nautical saying—it's a way of life. In this chapter, we've sailed through the many shades of adaptability: from the sudden squalls to the subtle breeze changes, from pivoting to rerouting, from storm-proofing to holding the rudder steady.

Adaptability doesn't always shout. Sometimes, it whispers.

Throughout this chapter, we've explored moments where **changing course wasn't a weakness—it was wisdom**. Where trimming sails saved fuel, where preparing ahead of time saved lives and cargo, and where pivoting around danger kept the voyage on track. We've seen how true strength lies not in rigidity, but in the graceful balance between **resistance and surrender**.

You read the sky.

You feel the current.

You trim, reef, and adjust.

And keep moving forward—sometimes slowly, sometimes sideways—but always with intent, holding the steering firmly, using the rudder as needed.

So, if you're facing a change, you didn't ask for… a career shift, a relationship twist, a sudden storm in your health or finances… remember this:

You are the captain. You still hold the helm.

Keep your sails trimmed. Keep your eyes on the horizon.

And never stop navigating your life with wisdom, courage, and grace.

CHAPTER 4

MAINTAIN THE HULL BEFORE IT LEAKS – THE DISCIPLINE OF SMALL CHECKS

Part 1: The Daily Rounds — Spot Trouble Early

There's a saying at sea: **a small leak can sink a great ship**. It may not happen in a day or a week, but if ignored, even the tiniest crack can spell disaster. That's why on board a vessel; daily rounds aren't just a routine—they're a lifeline.

I remember clearly the days when I was a young third officer. Back then, I was full of energy and eager to learn the ropes of shipboard life. One of our daily responsibilities, especially during night hours when the engine room was unmanned, was to carry out engine room rounds. Every four hours like clockwork, we'd descend into that maze of metal and machinery, guided by torchlight and training, ears alert for unfamiliar sounds and eyes sharp for anything out of place.

One particular night is etched in my memory. It was a routine round—nothing unusual on the surface. The sea was calm, and everything on the bridge was steady. I made my way down to the engine room, clipboard in hand, ticking off checkpoints one by one. But as I walked past the generator space, something caught my eye.

A faint mist shimmered under the inspection light. I leaned in closer and saw it—a thin jet of fuel spraying from a pinhole in the fuel line. It was under high pressure, nearly invisible unless viewed from the right direction. The worst part? It was spraying dangerously close to a hot surface. Around me, there were high-speed rotating parts, hot exhaust manifolds, and electrical circuits that could have easily turned this tiny spray into a full-blown fireball.

My heart raced.

I quickly alerted the duty engineer, who ran down and changed over the affected generator. The line was repaired, the area cleaned, and just like that, the danger was gone. But that night left a lasting lesson in my heart—**prevention doesn't shout; it whispers.** It's up to us to listen.

The Power of Preventive Routines

Ships are floating cities with thousands of components operating in harmony. For that harmony to remain intact, every small part must be monitored. That's why daily inspections are sacred. We check for loose bolts, unusual vibrations, odd smells, or leaks—anything that signals a problem in the making.

Similarly, in our personal lives, daily rounds can be just as vital.

- In **health**, it might be paying attention to your sleep patterns, how you feel when you wake up, your energy levels, or a small pain that keeps recurring.
- In **finances**, it could be tracking spending, noticing rising bills, or watching for a drop in savings.
- In **relationships**, it might mean observing emotional distance, communication patterns, or unexplained tension.

When you notice these small shifts early, you give yourself time to act before things spiral. Just like that pinhole in the fuel line, the earlier you catch it, the simpler the fix.

From Checklists to Check-ins

Onboard, we had checklists for every round—systems to ensure nothing got missed. While you may not have a printed form for life's daily checks, creating a habit of self-inquiry works the same way.

Now think for a moment. Ask yourself simple questions:

- Did anything feel off in my body today?
- Did I spend within my means?
- Did I nourish my relationships?
- Did I feel unusually anxious or tired?

These small self-checks are your personal daily rounds. Do these self-checks every night before you sleep. If you do it consistently, they give you control over your own "engine room." And more importantly, they help you prevent the metaphorical fire from ever starting.

Routine is Not Boring—It's Strategic

There's a misconception that routine kills creativity or spontaneity. At sea, we know the opposite is true. Routines are what keep the ship safe, allowing us to explore new destinations with confidence. Without Routines, we'd be adrift in chaos.

Routines around health, spending, learning, and connection create a foundation. From there, you can soar, try new things, and take healthy risks—because your hull is solid.

Think of your body as the ship, your mind as the engine room, and your choices as the rudder. When you do your daily rounds, you're not just maintaining—you're commanding like a Captain.

Lessons from a Young Officer

That night in the engine room taught me a lesson no classroom ever could. It wasn't a big emergency. No alarms blared. No chaos erupted. It was a quiet, nearly invisible hazard—caught only because I followed a simple routine with sincerity.

Sometimes, life's biggest victories come from the crises we *never* have to face—because we were prepared, attentive, and present.

You don't have to be perfect. You just have to show up consistently. Do your rounds. Ask the right questions. Look beneath the surface. Whether you're checking health issues or your own stress levels, small inspections prevent big disasters.

Discipline saves lives. Attention prevents regret. Prevention is power.

So, before the hull leaks—inspect. Before burnout—rest. Before overspending—review. Before sickness—check-in.

You don't need to be in a crisis to take action. You only need to care enough to look closely.

Your ship—your life—is worth it.

Part 2: The Engine Room Isn't Glamorous — But It Keeps You Going

The bridge of the ship is sleek and clean, offering panoramic views of the open sea. It's where cadets dream of someday commanding, and where the illusion of glamour lives. But every captain knows that the real lifeblood of the ship lies far below—in the belly of the beast. In the engine room.

Hot, loud, and often suffocating in the summer heat that can reach nearly 50°C, the engine room doesn't get much praise. It's not where medals are earned or photographs are taken. But it is where voyages are made or broken.

I remember my early days onboard, still new to the responsibilities of a junior officer. I would head down for safety rounds, stepping into the bowels of the ship where the temperature and humidity felt like stepping into a steam sauna. Every bolt, valve, pump, and pipe had a role, and each needed to be monitored, oiled, adjusted—or else.

There's a kind of rhythm in an engine room, the constant thrum of machinery, the hiss of steam, the occasional clank of a spanner tightening a stubborn nut. I watched the engineers, faces slick with sweat, sleeves rolled up, moving from engine to compressor, from purifier to generator, often without a word. Their silence wasn't indifference—it was focus.

They didn't need recognition. They understood a simple truth: **you don't need glory when your job is to keep things running.**

A Lesson in Heat and Discipline

One summer, somewhere in the South China Sea, our vessel was steaming through scorching weather. Outside, the sky was blue, and the ocean was calm. But inside, below deck, the temperature was unforgiving. I was there for safety rounds. The Second Engineer was doing routine maintenance on the auxiliary engines.

Sweat pooled beneath his hard hat. His overalls clung to our backs. The heat seemed to rise from the floor like a living thing. The air was thick and heavy with the smell of oil, metal, and salt. Every movement was slow, deliberate. Even lifting a spanner felt like a heavy job.

Yet, there was no complaint. The work had to be done—timely maintenance of lube oil pumps, checks on pressure gauges, filter cleaning, and alignment checks—all part of the day's schedule. Delaying even one task could mean cascading failures later on.

You see, **onboard, there's no postponing. No, I'll do it tomorrow.'** Because tomorrow, you might be in the middle of a squall, short of hands, or dealing with a mechanical emergency. Everything must be maintained as planned. Everything must be ready, every day.

This taught me a powerful life lesson: **The most essential work in your life is often the least glamorous.** The world may praise charisma, talent, and spotlight achievements, but it's the invisible discipline—your diet, your workouts, your sleep, your budgeting, your quiet perseverance—that truly propels you forward.

The Quiet Power of the Unseen

A ship doesn't move because the captain gives a command. It moves because someone has tightened the fuel injectors, checked the cylinder pressures, and ensured the cooling water is flowing. It moves because someone spent hours in the heat changing filters, greasing bearings, and cleaning bilges.

Life is much the same.

We like to focus on outcomes—weight loss, promotions, and investments maturing. But those results are only the tip of the iceberg. The real engine is your daily discipline.

Just as ships have PMS—Planned Maintenance Systems—we need personal maintenance systems too.

- **For your health:** routine checkups, proper hydration, exercise, and rest.
- **For your finances:** budget checks, expense tracking, debt management, savings.
- **For your mind:** mental breaks, journaling, reflection, seeking help when needed.

– In our lives, our "engine rooms" are often neglected. We get caught up in surface-level busyness and ignore what's powering our journey. We forget that burnout, a silent heart attack, a mounting credit card bill, or a mental breakdown doesn't announce itself—it creeps in when we're too distracted by the noise above.

Discipline Over Motivation

Motivation is fickle—it comes and goes like the tide. But **discipline is your anchor.** No matter how tired you are, how hot it is, or how thankless the job is, discipline keeps the ship moving.

I've seen engineers at sea give up their sleep just to overhaul a pump because it was leaking at 2 a.m. I've seen oiler boys wipe every drip tray spotless before bunkering, just to prevent any safety risk. They didn't wait to feel inspired. They knew that small lapses could lead to big losses.

In life, you don't wait to feel like saving money—you automate your savings – allocating part of your salary, every month, little by little, keeping it aside. You don't wait to feel energized to exercise—you must show up in the gymnasium anyway. You don't wait to feel spiritual to pray or meditate—you must make it part of your daily rhythm.

No Excuses—Find the Time

Some people say, "I don't have time."

It's not about time. It's about priorities.

You don't delay oiling a bearing because the engine is too busy running. You find a safe window and you do it—because if you don't, the damage will cost you much more. In the same way, don't delay tending to your emotional well-being, your relationships, or your finances. Find the window. Act before breakdown. Whether it's your body, your marriage, your work ethic, or your inner peace, **you maintain it not for show, but for survival.**

The True Measure of Readiness

We used to say, "If the engine room is silent, something's wrong." A running ship hums, roars, and vibrates with energy. And if anything sounds off—even a subtle change—you act fast.

That's how you must treat your own life.

Are you running too quietly? Feeling disconnected, uninspired, and exhausted? Something may be off in your engine room. Maybe it's time for a small service check: eat better, sleep longer, speak to your soul mate, and breathe deeper.

You don't need to overhaul everything at once. But start with the basics—**fuel, pressure, temperature, rhythm.** In life terms: healthy food, rest, vacation, hydration, and habits that keep you aligned.

Don't neglect the unglamorous side of life. Discipline is maintenance. Maintenance is movement. Movement is life.

And always remember—when the ship arrives safely at port, it's not just the captain who gets the credit. It's the quiet hands in the engine room who showed up day after day, in silence and sweat, to keep the heart of the vessel beating strong.

Part 3: Rust Never Sleeps — Neither Should You

The first thing every sailor learns on deck is this: **the sea is beautiful, but it's also relentless**. The salt in the air, the moisture in the wind—these aren't just poetic elements. They're corrosive forces, slowly eating away at the steel of the ship. And if you aren't vigilant, one day, you'll find your trusted vessel weeping rust, silently falling apart from within.

I remember early in my career, as a young Chief Officer on a cargo vessel bound for Kingston, Jamaica, I was overseeing the deck maintenance crew. It was late spring, and the sea had been kind—no storms, no swells, just smooth sailing. I thought we could afford to ease up a bit on the routine deck chipping and painting schedule. After all, we had just painted those areas a few months back.

But then one morning during my daily walk around, I saw it—**tiny orange freckles blooming beneath a layer of paint** near the forecastle deck. It was a small area, no bigger than my palm. I made a mental note to get it sorted the next day. **But the next day became the next week. By the time we returned from Kingston and a few other American ports, a month later, the rust had spread like wildfire.** What was once a minor touch-up job became a major repair task. The steel beneath had started pitting, weakening the structure.

That was the day I learned a lesson I never forgot: **rust never sleeps**. And neither should we—not when it comes to maintenance, and not when it comes to life.

The Silent Erosion of Neglect

In life, rust wears a different coat. It might look like skipping your morning walk for "just one day." Or putting off that call to a loved one. It may look simple, nothing dramatic at first glance. But it starts a pattern. And patterns are like currents, carry us far—either in the right direction or dangerously off course.

Maintenance, whether of a ship or a life, is not about grand acts. It's about **the unglamorous, uncelebrated consistency** that holds everything together.

The Hull and Your Habits

Imagine your life as a vessel. Your habits are the hull—the part that stays submerged, hidden from the world, but is responsible for keeping you afloat. What happens if you stop inspecting it? What if you assume, because it's out of sight, it's also safe?

Let me give you another glimpse into sea life. Onboard, we have something called a "hull survey." It's a thorough inspection where divers in port or surveyors in dry dock assess the condition of the submerged hull. It's tedious, expensive, and time-consuming. But we do it because the alternative—"hull failure"—is catastrophic.

Your own habits need the same kind of surveying. Your **health, your finances, your relationships, your sleep, your attitude**—they need regular inspection. Don't wait until something cracks or breaks. Don't wait for the heart scare, the overdue bills, the sleepless nights, or the broken trust.

What you ignore today becomes your storm tomorrow.

Sweat Today, Sail Smooth Tomorrow

During one voyage in the Indian Ocean, I worked with a Bosun named Mathews—gritty, experienced, and wise in the way only sea veterans can be. He was relentless with maintenance. "We chip, we prime, we paint—every week," he would say. "Even if the deck looks clean, rust is always hiding."

His routine was painful at the moment. Long hours in the sun, sweating in coveralls, brush in one hand, scraper in the other. But months later, while other vessels struggled with deck corrosion in the monsoon season, ours stood strong. Mathews didn't just prevent rust—he preserved our vessel's integrity. Quietly. Day by day.

That's how habits work, too.

Going for a morning walk. Drinking water. Reviewing your expenses. Talking to your spouse. Going for a walk with your loved ones, having a conversation with your friend over a coffee, saying "no" to that extra slice of cake. **These aren't dramatic changes. But they're your "Mathews moments".** They're how you preserve the ship of your life, not for today's calm, but for tomorrow's storm.

The Financial Hull

Financially speaking, debt is rust. Impulsive purchases and delayed payments as you do by credit cards. It starts small— "just one dinner out," or "I'll pay it off next month." But that small amount becomes multiplied in the coming weeks. That one late payment dents your credit score.

We "Log" everything on board, not because we love numbers, but because **ignorance is costly**.

Apply the same principle to your personal finances. Track your spending like you'd track a leak. Audit your bank statements. Clean up your unwanted subscriptions like you'd scrape rust. Not glamorous, but essential.

Emotional Rust Is Real

There's another kind of rust that's more dangerous than financial or physical. **Emotional rust.** That slow bitterness that builds up when a conversation is left unsaid. When forgiveness is delayed. When stress is ignored, saying a simple sorry is strenuous.

In real life, a misunderstanding between soul mates slows down effectiveness. Tempers flare. Morale dips. But when we sit together, over a coffee, clear the air—it's like applying a fresh coat of paint. Your ship doesn't just look better. It works better.

Your heart, your relationships—they too need upkeep. A "thank you" often said. A "sorry" that didn't wait. These are your tools. Use them before rust sets in.

Procrastination Is Saltwater

The truth is, procrastination is like saltwater in the air—**invisible, but always present**. It settles on every surface, waiting for a lapse. And like rust, it sets in when inactive.

It's easy to say, "I'll start tomorrow." That gym routine. That apology. That thank you. That praise. That walk. That candlelight dinner. That gazing at black velvet dusted with millions of stars. That health checkup. But every delay is like missing one round in your engine room.

One time, I witnessed a delay that almost cost us dearly. A fuel line was reported with a slight leak, but was marked "non-urgent." A few weeks later, the leak worsened and led to downtime in the middle of a critical cargo operation. Hours of delay. Financial penalties. All because we let a small rust spot grow into a hole.

Delay is not neutral—it's decay in disguise.

Paint Your Ship Daily

Every ship, no matter how majestic, needs painting. Whether you're a CEO or a student, a parent or a sailor, we all need upkeep. Paint your ship **daily**—with good choices, small actions, honest conversations, and mindful routines.

Let rust fear you, not the other way around.

Inspect your ship before it creaks. Walk the decks of your own life. The more you maintain, the less you'll need to repair. That's the Captain's code.

Part 4: Dry Dock Days — Sometimes You Must Stop to Repair

A ship's strength is not proven only when it rides out the roughest waves. Its true durability is forged and fortified in the quiet, deliberate days spent in dry dock—those rare times when it is lifted out of the water, taken off its path, and given the care it truly needs.

The Dry Dock Ritual

Every two to five years, depending on the type of vessel and trading patterns, a ship is brought into dry dock. It's an extraordinary process. The massive steel hull that usually disappears beneath the sea is finally exposed, allowing engineers and inspectors to examine every inch for corrosion, cracks, and wear. These are areas we can't see—or safely access—while the ship is afloat.

I remember standing on the bridge wing, watching water drain away from the dock like an ebbing tide. Slowly, the mighty ship settled onto her blocks. She stood there, still and proud, her massive propeller now visible to human eyes, rudder fixed in place like the spine of a resting giant.

The ship had been through storms, long voyages, harsh waters, scorching summers, and frigid winters. From above, everything had looked fine. But down below? That was a different story.

As the hull was scraped, cleaned, and inspected, the scars of sea life came into view—patches of rust where the paint had thinned, worn anodes that no longer offered protection, and sea valves that had visible sea growths. The truth was clear: no matter how well she performed at sea, this vessel—like every one of us—needed care beyond the surface.

A Pause Is Not Weakness

In life, many people keep sailing through without pause. They push ahead, month after month, project after project, responsibility after responsibility. But just like a ship, we need scheduled maintenance too. And that's where the concept of "dry dock days" becomes vital.

These are the intentional pauses in life when we stop the outward voyage to tend to our inner workings. It might be a vacation, a weekend retreat, a digital detox, a dinner with a loved one, an evening spent alone looking at millions of glittering stars, or even a few hours spent unplugged in nature. Whatever form it takes, this pause is not a luxury—it's a necessity.

Let me take you back to a time when I failed to heed this lesson.

My Personal Burnout

I was sailing continuously for months, juggling the daily command responsibilities of a large container ship. Crew changes, cargo schedules, audits, machinery issues, spare parts, port state inspections, surveys—you name it, one after another. I told myself I had no time to rest. **An old saying, "A Captain never sleeps," became a reality.** Sleep became shorter, meals more rushed, and my patience wore thinner by the day.

Then one night, while going through pre-arrival checks before entering a congested port, I found myself blanking out in front of the radar screen. My mind had simply stopped working for a moment—like a computer freezing up. That had never happened before.

Luckily, my second officer was there. He noticed something was wrong and gently offered to continue the navigation. I stepped out to the bridge wing, breathed in the salt air, and realized I was exhausted and drained.

That moment became my signal. I needed a dry dock. Not tomorrow. Now.

At the end of that voyage, I applied for leave and permitted myself to fully disconnect—no emails, no work calls, no responsibility other than to rest and recover. I had uninterrupted and peaceful sleep like I hadn't in months. I took long walks. I read books unrelated to ships or schedules. I even learned to cook a new dish.

The result? When I returned to the sea after a few months, I was sharper, calmer, and more present. Like a ship emerging from a dry dock with a fresh coat of paint and a humming engine, I was renewed.

Maritime Truths, Life Lessons

Here's the thing: no matter how strong a vessel is, it cannot ignore dry dock. Regulatory bodies require it. Insurance companies demand it. Why? Because unseen damage is still damage. And damage ignored becomes a disaster.

So why do we, in our personal lives, think we can keep going without repair?

Your hull is your body. Your engine is your mind and heart. Your valves are your financial systems, relationships, and emotional channels. Each of them needs time off the water to be restored.

Just like stress fractures form on metal under repetitive strain, your resilience suffers micro-tears from continuous pressure. And just like biofouling slows a ship down, so too does clutter—mental, physical, digital—drag your performance.

Dry Dock isn't about indulgence. It's about prevention. And prevention is always cheaper than repair.

Let's plan your dry dock.

Now take a moment, before you proceed further. I request you to close your eyes and think for a moment about your last dry dock. When was it? Is it so far distant that you cannot even recall?

Then, it's the time. You need time off the water—to be restored.

Schedule It. Don't Wait for Crisis.

Right now you mark your calendar for breaks—real ones, not just weekends filled with chores.

Make It Thorough.

Use your rest period to review every corner of your life. How's your physical health? Emotional well-being? Are you saving enough? Are your relationships nurtured?

Let the World Wait.

Don't fall into the trap of thinking your worth is tied to constant output. Real productivity flows from restoration.

Celebrate the Tranquillity of Stillness.

Let that peace sweep over your life. Let your mind breathe. That's where ideas, gratitude, and healing grow.

In your dry dock, you are not idle. You are rebuilding. If you allow yourself to rest. Be it a challenge in your career, a change in your personal life, or simply another week of responsibilities—you will sail with a strong hull, a clean rudder, and a heart full of enthusiasm.

Take the pause. The sea will wait.

The Ship You Sail Deserves Your Daily Care

There's a kind of quiet confidence that comes from a well-kept ship, be it a dry dock or just preventive maintenance. That's peace of mind—and it doesn't happen by accident.

It's the result of discipline. Of daily rounds. Of routine maintenance. Of facing small issues before they become large ones. It's choosing to act before the storm, not during it.

And so it is with life.

You cannot sail safely for long without constant, disciplined upkeep.

This chapter revealed what most people ignore: through early inspections, sweaty maintenance, and routine discipline. You've seen it through the quiet engine room, through the corrosion hidden under fresh paint, and through the emotional "bilge" that, if left unattended, corrodes even the strongest soul.

Now ask yourself — are you walking the decks of your own life daily? Or are you waiting for something to break before you take action?

Prevention doesn't shout. It whispers. And it's up to you to listen.

Stop romanticizing the chaos of last-minute firefighting. Stop believing rest is a luxury. Whether it's your physical health, your finances, your relationships, or your emotional core — "*everything good in life is built on quiet, sustained care*".

- Do your rounds.
- Sweat in maintenance, so you don't bleed in crisis.
- Know that self-discipline is self-respect.
- Create a rhythm in your routine — even when no one is watching.

Your daily choices are the paint that protects your steel. Your habits are the bolts and welds that hold your life together. Your rest is not laziness — it's a dry dock for the soul.

And let's be clear: the world doesn't reward the flashiest ship. It rewards the one who arrives — whole, steady, strong, and safe. That can only happen if you **maintain the hull before it leaks**.

So don't wait.

Analyze it now. Jot it down and act on it.

Your life is your vessel.

And every bit of care pays off.

Sail strong, Captain. The next port awaits.

CHAPTER 5

ALWAYS HAVE A LIFEBOAT — THE POWER OF A BACKUP PLAN

AA wise sailor knows that even the sturdiest ship can face disaster. That's why lifeboats are always ready. In life, too, having backup plans—emergency funds, contingency strategies, and emotional safety nets—can mean the difference between sinking and surviving.

Part 1: The Lifeboat Is Always Ready — Preparing Before You Need It

Out at sea, there is one piece of equipment that every mariner hopes to never use but is trained to depend on without question: **the lifeboat.**

When you walk the deck of a ship—whether a sleek container vessel slicing through the Pacific or an aging tanker in the Indian Ocean—you'll notice the lifeboat is secured nicely. They aren't ornamental. They're not there for show. They are lifelines. Literally.

Before we ever leave port, the lifeboats are checked. Weekly and monthly, they're inspected. Every three months, they're lowered and tested. The crew is trained relentlessly—abandon ship drills, life jacket donning, life raft, and Lifeboat launching procedures. We prepare as if the worst might happen at any moment. Because at sea, you don't get second chances. And most importantly, the more prepared you are, the less likely you'll ever need to use the lifeboat.

This mindset—preparing before the storm hits, before the crisis knocks—holds a deep lesson not just for life at sea, but for life ashore.

The Lifeboat Mindset: Be Ready Before You Need

I remember sailing through the rough waters of the North Atlantic one winter. We were en route to Shimizu, cutting through ice-laced waves near Kamchatka, Russia, under a steel-grey sky.

The temperature had dropped, the wind stabbed the skin like a thousand needles, and the sea showed no mercy.

As a Captain of the vessel, I had a deep sense of responsibility for my crew and ship. Every detail mattered. Before we left the last port, Vancouver, we had the lifeboats lowered and tested as part of a 3-month routine. The crew went through abandon ship drills after departure. Some may have rolled their eyes—they'd done this a hundred times. But it's a routine – a practice we never miss. Because you don't rehearse safety *after* the iceberg. You prepare *before*.

A few days into our voyage, we got hit by a brutal storm. Force 10 winds. Waves towering like mountains. The ship groaned as we pushed through. For a brief moment, we had a blackout, generators tripped. We lost power. My first thought? Are the lifeboats ready? Are we ready—just in case?

Thankfully, we recovered power within minutes. And that readiness gave me peace of mind even in the chaos. That's the essence of this chapter: **you don't build your lifeboat during the storm—you build it well before.**

Preparing Financial Lifeboats: Buffers and Bailouts

Let's bring this lesson to land.

Too many people live paycheck to paycheck, hoping things will go smoothly. But life—like the sea—isn't always smooth. There are layoffs. Medical emergencies. Accidents. Markets crash. Cars break down. Roofs leak. Loved ones fall ill.

Imagine being in the middle of financial turbulence and only then starting to think about savings. It's like realizing your lifeboat is missing after the ship has already begun to sink.

In our maritime world, we have spare parts for almost everything—an extra pump, backup generators, redundant systems. It's costly, yes, but essential. A single backup pump can mean the difference between a functioning engine room and a drifting, powerless ship in the deep ocean or in pirated waters.

Financially, your emergency fund is that backup pump. It's your lifeboat.

Here's how you build it:

- **Start savings how small it is:** Start saving as soon as possible, even with a small amount. Be consistent. Continue and try to increase the amount by ten percent every year. When you have savings of about one month of expenses, is a win. Then aim for three and then six months.
- **Creating an emergency fund:** When you have savings of one year of expenses, that's your emergency fund – that's your lifeboat, do not use it for anything else, unless an emergency.
- **Life Insurance:** Life insurance isn't a luxury—it's lifeboats; you pay timely to keep ready.
- **Health Insurance:** Health insurance for you and your loved ones is essential. Check all documents carefully and take a good one that covers everything in case of a medical emergency. Make sure the premium never fails.

- **Multiple income streams:** Like having dual engines, side hustles, or passive income sources can carry you when the main engine fails.
- **Contingency planning:** What if you lost your job tomorrow? Do you know your lifeboat drill? Can you survive ninety days without sinking? Plan in advance and write it down.

Preparing financially is not about fear—it's about freedom. It's knowing that if the storm hits, you won't be overwhelmed. You'll still be afloat.

Emotional Lifeboats: Anchors in Rough Waters

But storms don't just come in the form of unpaid bills. They come in grief, heartbreak, depression, loneliness, and burnout. Emotional storms can be just as devastating, and can be worse than financial breakdowns—and we must prepare for them too.

Think of your emotional lifeboats as:

- **Friendships you nurture before you need them.**
- **Journaling or meditation practices that anchor your mind.**
- **Professional help—therapists, counselors—you've established contact with in calm times.**
- **Spiritual beliefs or faith that give you comfort.**

You Are the Captain. Don't Sail Without a Lifeboat.

So, build your lifeboat. Test it. Maintain it. Train with it. And then? Go sail with confidence. Because the sea will rise. The storms will come. **But you, Captain, will be ready.**

Part 2: Fire Drills and Sea Drills — Rehearse for the Worst to Sail Through It

There's a sound that slices through the quiet rhythm of life at sea—the shrill, urgent ring of the general alarm. It's not something any sailor comes to love, but it's something we all learn to respect. That sound means only one thing: Time to move. It's either an emergency or a drill.

Why We Drill When There's No Fire

Every ship I've commanded had a rhythm, and part of that rhythm was discipline. We drilled—rain or shine, smooth voyage, or choppy seas. Fire drills, abandon ship drills, oil spill response drills, and man overboard drills—each had its own scenario and protocol. And none of them were optional.

I remember once, during a calm passage through the Indian Ocean, during an internal audit, I was asked to order a fire drill at 2200 hours, to check if the crew was ready, well past the evening meal. My second officer looked at me like I had lost my bearings. "Captain," he said, "it's peaceful. Nothing's wrong. Why now?"

Exactly. Because nothing was wrong.

We simulated a fire in the engine control room. The crew scrambled—some still chewing their last bite of dinner—into fire suits, breathing apparatus, and Oxygen checks. We mustered, responded, and critiqued the run. The whole event took less than 30 minutes.

Once, while sailing in the South China Sea, our fire alarm suddenly blared at 2:30 a.m. A fire had broken out in the galley-ship's kitchen, due to a malfunctioning oven. Thick smoke was spreading across the accommodation.

When the fire broke out in the galley, no one froze. No one shouted aimlessly. The crew responded with precision. It was like watching a well-rehearsed play unfold—each role executed, every movement intentional. Within minutes, the fire was suppressed and the situation was controlled.

You don't drill because disaster is certain. You drill so disaster doesn't destroy you.

Financial Fire Drills — Play the Worst Case Before It Happens

Too many of us walk through life like junior officers grumbling during a drill. We assume that "all is well" will last forever. But as I've learned both on the bridge and on land, emergencies don't announce themselves.

Financial hardship is the modern fire—sudden, spreading, and unforgiving. One leak in the system—a job loss, a market dip, a medical emergency—and your entire vessel can begin to tilt.

That's why you drill in peace.

Here's how to conduct a financial fire drill:

- **Track Your Essentials:** Just like we log the daily fuel, lube oil, and freshwater levels on board, you must know what it costs to run your household. Create a clear list of your non-negotiables—housing, food, utilities, and healthcare.

- **Simulate Income Loss:** Just as we simulate the loss of steering or power, ask yourself—Can I survive three months without my main income? Could I pivot quickly? If not, it's time to build that reserve.
- **Check Your Safety Gear:** Check your insurance—health, life, and home. Understand what's covered and what's not. Don't wait for the blaze to realize your extinguisher is missing.
- **Know Your Financial Exits:** Onboard, we know every escape route. You must know your own—what expenses can be cut immediately? What funds or assets can be accessed in a crisis?
- **Brief the Crew:** Your family is your ship's crew. They must be included. Discuss what steps to take if something happens to you. Involve them in your budgeting and backup plans.

One of my shipmates once faced a sudden layoff when his company shut down an entire regional office. He had no savings. He told me later, "I had a good job, a new car, and a house mortgage. But I didn't have a lifeboat." Within two months, he was selling possessions just to make rent.

That hardship became his wake-up call. Today, he maintains one year's worth of emergency funds, multiple income streams, and a leaner lifestyle. "Now," he says, "I run fire drills for my bank account."

Emotional Fire Drills — Prepare for Stormy Waters

Emotional breakdowns are often quieter than financial crises but can be more dangerous. A sudden death in the family. A bitter breakup. A betrayal by someone you trusted. These aren't hypothetical scenarios—you all are sailing through one or the other.

The problem? Most of us have no emotional life vests.

We don't journal until we're overwhelmed.

We don't talk to friends until we're drowning.

We don't say "no" until we're stretched thin.

So, how do we rehearse emotionally?

- **Journal your daily inspection** round in a diary every night before bed. It helps you understand where you're rusting silently—resentments, fears, insecurities.
- Boundaries are your fire doors. **Practice saying "no"** before you're buried under "yes."
- Feedback is your radar. **Trusted friends can tell you where you're drifting** off course before you hit something.
- Support networks are your emergency response team. **Cultivate friends, mentors, or professionals** long before the storm hits.
- Recovery habits—**Meditation, walks, music, or prayer**—are your breathing apparatus. Don't wait until you can't breathe to use them.

Drill emotionally, and when the squalls of life come, you won't capsize—you'll stay the course.

The Calm Between Drills Is the Time to Prepare

When everything is peaceful, that's when most people forget to prepare. But that's the exact time to plan.

Repetition Builds Confidence

There's a funny thing about repetition—it doesn't just build skill. It builds confidence.

When you've practiced your moves dozens of times, fear has less grip. You can move without hesitation, without doubt.

Rehearse calmly, and you'll respond like a professional when chaos comes.

Your Captain's Call:

- Drill in calm to act in crisis.
- Practice in peace to perform under pressure.
- Prepare not because the storm is certain—but so you can sail through it when it comes.

That's the mariner's wisdom.

That's the sailor's soul.

That's The Captain's Code.

Part 3: Redundant Systems — Why Smart Ships Have Backup for the Backup

The Ocean Doesn't Forgive a Single Point of Failure

The sea has no patience for excuses. If a ship's engine fails in the middle of the Pacific, it won't wait politely while you figure things out. If your navigation system goes down near a busy strait, the sea won't shift its tides to make life easier. It will just keep moving—relentless, indifferent, and vast.

That's why every ship worth her salt is built with redundancy in mind.

- Onboard, there's a backup for nearly every vital system. Engine controls are doubled. Two or more generators run in shifts, ready to take over if another fails. Steering gears have two pumps and emergency steering. Emergency lighting kicking in instantly if the main power supply cuts out. There are even ships with multiple bridge control stations—if one fails, the ship can still be maneuvered from another.

This isn't just technical flair. It's a lifeline. I've seen firsthand how these systems save lives.

One Night in the South China Sea

Let me take you back on a voyage through the South China Sea. It was a humid afternoon—visibility was poor, the radar screen was flickering with echoes, and the sky was cloaked in low clouds. We were exiting a congested TSS (Traffic Separation Scheme) route with heavy crossing traffic and fishing fleets. Suddenly, the steering alarm rang. The rudder is not responding. We rang the general alarm and made announcements. My Chief Engineer immediately activated the changeover system to connect the emergency steering, and within a minute, the emergency steering system came alive, and we regained steering. We had trained for this. We managed to steer through heavy traffic. In the meantime, the Electrical Engineer looked at the main steering, and within the next hour, we restored the main steering system.

Had we relied on a single system, that afternoon could've gone very differently.

That experience etched a lasting truth in me:

Redundancy isn't about pessimism—it's about preparedness.

Financial Redundancy — Don't Sail with Just One Engine

Back on land, many people sail through life with only one financial "engine"—a single income stream. It's usually a job. And as long as that job runs well, life moves forward. But what happens when that engine fails?

A company restructures. A global event shuts down industries. Illness strikes. Suddenly, the engine coughs, sputters, and dies.

And life? Life has to keep moving like a ship.

We need to build redundant systems into our finances.

Multiple Streams of Income

Consider any of these ideas to start your side income journey. Take it seriously. Like setting a small sail, it may not seem like much at first — but with steady winds and direction, it can carry you far over time.

- A small freelance gig alongside your full-time job.
- A properly guided Investment in mutual funds or the share market.
- A rental property.
- A monetized hobby—art, tutoring, writing, consulting.

Skills and Cross-Training — Your Alternative Propulsion

On a ship, every officer learns the other officer's job. If one man is down, the ship can still function.

Your skills are like that. Maybe you're an accountant, but can you teach? Design? Write? Speak another language?

Invest in yourself. Attend workshops or webinars. Get certifications. Expand your range. The more "engines" you have, the smoother you'll sail—even through storms.

Emotional Redundancy — More Than One Anchor

If conditions worsen or the seabed is unpredictable, a second anchor is dropped. That's emotional redundancy—having more than one thing that grounds you.

When one support fails, the others hold you fast.

Diversify Your Support Network

If your emotional world revolves around just one person—a partner, a parent, a best friend—what happens if they're unavailable, or hurting too?

Build a fleet of connections:

- Old friends who knew you before your success.
- Mentors who challenge your thinking.
- Peers who understand your current struggles.
- The family that grounds you in who you are.

Take a notebook, close your eyes, and figure out who those people are, write down their names, and get in touch with them. Speak to them from time to time, and build a relationship.

In life, create your mental emergency manual:

- Who do I call when I feel overwhelmed?
- What 3 actions calm me immediately?
- What phrases or prayers remind me of my strength?

Write it down. Train yourself to use it.

Your Captain's Call

- Build financial backups before you need them.
- Keep multiple emotional anchors—not just one.
- Learn new skills, even when your old ones serve you well.
- Practice your habits of calm every day—they'll save you when storms hit.

The sea does not care for excuses. But it respects preparation.

So, sail like a smart ship—with backup for your backup.

Part 4: Don't Wait for Distress Signals — Recognize Early Signs

At Sea, Small Signs Speak Loudly

The sea doesn't shout. It whispers.

Long before disaster strikes a ship, the signs are already there—quiet, subtle, and often easy to overlook. The sharp ear of a seasoned mariner catches them: an unusual hum from the engine room, a slight delay in the hydraulic steering, the faint smell of something burning in an electrical panel, or a low reading on a pressure gauge.

Every ship I've sailed on, from my cadet days to my command years, has taught me this fundamental truth: **the ocean is merciless, but never entirely silent. It always speaks. You just have to listen.**

I remember an incident during a Pacific crossing. It was a clear morning, and we were a few days out of Yokohama, heading toward the US West Coast. I was still a young Chief Officer then, doing my usual rounds after breakfast. As I walked past the No. 3 cargo hold, I noticed a rhythmic *pinging* sound—not loud, not alarming, but odd. No one else had heard it yet.

Instead of ignoring it, I called the bosun, and we did a closer inspection. We found a hairline crack on the hatch coaming. It had started to stress under the constant flex of loaded conditions and sea swell. One big wave could have worsened it, letting seawater in and risking cargo damage.

We temporarily reinforced it immediately and avoided a major problem. Vigilance doesn't cost much—but negligence can cost everything.

Good seafarers don't wait for distress signals. They act at the first whisper.

Financial Warning Signs — Reading the Sea of Your Wallet

Life ashore, especially in our finances, is not much different. Financial breakdowns rarely come out of nowhere. They build up silently, layer by layer, until the structure buckles.

Skipping Savings is Your First Alarm Bell

Let's say you've stopped saving regularly. "Just this month," you say. Then next month, there's an unexpected bill. Then, the car needs repair. Suddenly, it's been six months since you put anything aside.

You're not in distress yet. But the whispers have begun.

Reliance on One Income source

If the first sputter, do you have anything to fall back on?

Mounting Debt = Taking on Water

Debt is not inherently bad— but if your credit card bill is growing and you're only paying the minimum, or if personal loans are stacking up, you're taking on water. It won't feel urgent, but beneath the surface, your stability is being eroded.

This is the whisper, listen to it.

Every small action plugs a leak.

Emotional Red Flags — The Inner Hull

We all carry an invisible emotional hull, and like a ship's steel plating, it can withstand a lot—but not forever.

Persistent Fatigue

Fatigue is not laziness. It's a distress signal.

If you're constantly tired, emotionally drained, or dreading each new day—it's time to stop. Rest. Reassess.

Irritability Is the Screech of Emotional Bearings

When bearings start to wear out, you'll hear screeching or grinding. In humans, that's irritability.

If small things are making you snap—traffic, emails, loved ones—it's a sign you need lubrication: more rest, more laughter, more friends, more love, better boundaries.

Don't wait till your bearings are seized. Listen to the sound. Take early action.

Emotional Numbness

Apathy is the deadliest signal. When you stop caring about work, family, hobbies, yourself—it's like a rudderless ship drifting at sea.

You may still be moving, but there's no direction.

Don't ignore it. Get help. Talk to someone. Start a tiny routine—exercise, prayer, walking barefoot in the grass. Slowly, the rudder will return.

The Engineer's Golden Rule: Detect, Don't Deny

At sea, the best engineers and deck officers are not the ones who respond fastest—they're the ones who detect earliest.

Their secret? A habit of daily checks, sharp observation, and respect for silence.

That same habit can save your personal life. Make weekly check-ins part of your routine.

Ask yourself:

- Am I financially stressed this week?
- Did I feel joy at least once this week?
- Did I talk to someone who energizes me?
- Have I ignored something important for "later"?

Keep a journal. Not for perfection—just for pattern recognition.

The earlier you detect, the lighter your corrections.

Respond early. You are the captain of your own vessel.

Take action, however small. Seek help, however uncomfortable. Change course, however late.

Because the ocean doesn't forgive denial—but it rewards those who listen.

So, sail on, Captain. Eyes open. Ears tuned. Soul steady.

Your voyage has only begun.

Part 5: The Rescue Isn't Always Immediate — Stay Afloat Until Help Arrives

The Call for Help That Took Too Long

It was a bleak winter morning in the North Pacific, the kind where the sky swells with heavy grey clouds, and the wind hurls like an angry god. I was sailing as Captain aboard a container ship en route from Seattle to Yokohama. We were in the Gulf of Alaska when we received a distress signal near the Aleutian Islands —an EPIRB (Emergency Position-Indicating Radio Beacon) had been activated by a fishing vessel with 5 crew.

We contacted the rescue coordination center and immediately headed for the location of distress. But the location was about two days away.

The sea was churning—20-foot swells, sleet, and a wind chill that cut through even the thickest gloves. All we knew was that their engine had failed, and they were taking on water. The crew of that small vessel had only one mission now: **stay afloat.** I also remember wondering how they were coping—five souls alone in a cold ocean, clinging to a life raft, perhaps, with nothing but hope, preparation, and a few critical survival tools to keep them alive.

The next day, we were informed by the Rescue coordination center that another vessel had reached before us and found the inflated life raft, with the freezing, frightened, but alive crew. The boat had sunk by then. They had done exactly what every sailor must do in a crisis where rescue is delayed: **stay calm, stay afloat, and survive the moment.**

When the Storm Hits Your Life

There are times in life when distress comes unannounced. A sudden job loss. A major health diagnosis. A betrayal that cuts deep. An emergency expense you didn't see coming. And even after you've sent out your distress signal "mayday,"—told a friend, filed your claim, asked for help, **rescue may take time.**

Your boat might be sinking, but you still have to hold on.

This chapter isn't about fixing things instantly.

It's about enduring the space between crisis and solution. It's about the **lifeboat phase of survival**—when you're not where you were, but not yet safe either. It's about learning to keep your head above water until help arrives.

Even in the most advanced maritime operations, rescue is rarely immediate. Coast Guard vessels and helicopters have limitations—range, weather, and readiness. The EPIRB may trigger satellites instantly, but the response is hours or even days away.

In a survival situation, mental strength matters as much as physical preparedness.

Emergency Funds: Your Life-Raft

Those regular savings you built slowly, the ones that seemed boring to maintain when times were good—it becomes your raft in rough waters – it keeps you afloat for days and months. It buys you time to think clearly and act wisely.

Even if it only covers three months, that's three months of breathing room. Three months of groceries, rent, and sanity.

Side Hustles and Skills: Your Flotation Devices

Perhaps your main job is gone, but you've built other skills—freelancing, tutoring, writing, baking, and graphic design. These are the flotation devices you cling to while waiting for the next stable opportunity.

Reduce the Weight

During financial strain, you must cut unnecessary expenses. Pause subscriptions. Reevaluate priorities. It's not forever—but in crisis, lightness is survival – sustains you longer.

Emotional Lifeboats: When Healing Takes Time

It's the heart that's sinking. Loss. Loneliness. Heartbreak. Depression.

And just like at sea, help doesn't always arrive when you need it most.

You call a friend, but they're busy.

You see a therapist, but the appointment is next week.

You share your pain—but no one quite understands.

What do you do in that space?

You stay afloat.

Try the following:

- **Rituals Are Ropes** -Even simple routines—making your bed, walking in the park, lighting a candle at night—can be lifelines. They don't fix the storm, but they hold you steady. When I was going through a particularly hard time, I found solace in my morning tea ritual. It was absurdly simple—boiling water, pouring it slowly, watching the steam rise. But that tiny ritual anchored me. It reminded me that I was alive, that I was still here.

– **Calm is Contagious** In your own emotional storm, calm doesn't mean feeling anything—it means choosing to act with presence, not panic. Breathe. Speak slowly. Move deliberately. These small choices keep you from spiraling.

– **Hold On for One More Hour** You don't need to solve your crisis today. You just need to stay afloat today with all the backup you diligently prepared for months or years. Let tomorrow take care of itself.

– **The Power of Presence and Patience** Once, a junior officer under my command lost his mother while we were on a long voyage. He was devastated, and communication with the shore was limited. He came to me, eyes hollow, hands trembling. "I feel like I'm drowning, sir," he whispered. I didn't have a magic fix. I couldn't bring her back either. But I offered what I could—presence, routine, space, and listening. He kept doing his rounds. We ate meals together. He wrote his diary. And slowly, his grief softened—not vanished, but bearable. By the time we docked in Manzanillo, Panama, and arranged his flight back home, he was still grieving, but he was afloat.

Backup Plans Buy You Time, Not Perfection

The truth is, your emergency fund won't replace your salary. Your emotional rituals won't erase your pain. Your side hustle won't fully replace a lost career.

But that's not their job.

Their job is to buy you time.

Their job is to keep you breathing.

Their job is to carry you until the real rescue comes—be it a new opportunity, a healed heart, or simply a calmer season.

"We are not defined by how fast we are rescued, but by how long we can hold on."

Let your lifeboat carry you. Let your rituals anchor you. Let your plans hold you steady. The sea is wide—but so are you.

Backup Plans Are Anchors of Calm

Hope is not a strategy. A lifeboat is.

Every ship sails with the assumption that it might face a storm. And so, lifeboats are not optional—they're mandatory. Not because we expect to abandon ship, but because we must be ready if the unthinkable happens.

Life is no different.

Your emotional lifeboat might be a trusted friend, a journaling habit, or the deep breath you take before reacting. Your financial lifeboat might be a recurring deposit account or a mutual fund systematic investment plan, a side skill, or a clear budget. These things may seem small when the skies are clear, but in crisis, they become your anchor of calm.

Don't wait for life to knock the wind out of your sails. Build your lifeboats now. Create room in your budget, your routines, and your heart for things that steady you.

Because when the storm arrives—and it will—you won't panic. You won't drown. You'll float – for days and months, till the rescue arrives.

Now, take a moment. What's one backup you can build today—financial, emotional, or otherwise?

Don't wait for distress signals.

Be the captain of your life. And make sure your ship is ready—before the wind shifts.

CHAPTER 6

THERE IS NO TOMORROW – THE TIDE WAITS FOR NONE

The sea is in constant motion. Tides rise and fall, weather patterns shift and currents move unseen beneath the surface. A ship that delays casting off can miss its tide window, losing not just hours but opportunities. In life, as at sea, hesitation can cost far more than a delay—it can cost growth, progress, and purpose. This chapter is a call to act while the sea is still in your favor.

At sea, timing is everything. A missed tide means delay, danger, or even disaster. In life, hesitation, overthinking, and procrastination cost us opportunities, relationships, health, and progress. This chapter teaches the reader to move decisively, seize the moment, and develop the mindset of purposeful urgency.

Part 1: Miss the Tide, Miss the Voyage — Timing Is Everything

The Absolute Law of the Tide

There are moments at sea when you realize that time isn't just a clock—it's a force. I remember, when I was a Third Officer, a winter morning in the Port of Bristol, United Kingdom. Our ship was fully loaded. While carrying out the pre-departure tests, we found that one main engine part needed replacement, which may take about two hours. The engines were not ready we couldn't go.

Bristol is a tidal port with one of the highest tidal ranges in the world. If you miss your window during high tide, the next one available is only the next day. And when you're holding cargo deadlines and crew rotations, that delay can ripple through your whole voyage, and a lot of commercial pressure starts to develop apart from answering multiple emails relating to the missing tide.

We had to wait.

Timing, in maritime life, is non-negotiable. You cannot force the tide; you cannot argue with nature. You either act when the window opens—or miss the chance to sail.

This is one of the sea's greatest lessons: Opportunity is not always about preparation. It's also about timing.

The Illusion of the Perfect Moment

On land, unlike at sea, we are gifted with more comfort—and with it, more hesitation. How many times have you heard someone say:

- "I'll start saving when I make more money."
- "I'll go to the doctor when I have more time."
- "I'll tell you how I feel when the moment is right."
- "I'll switch careers when I'm 100% sure it'll work out."

The tide is high. The channel is open. The sky is clear. But we hesitate.

I once mentored a young seafarer who had immense potential. Smart, disciplined, good with people. He had an offer from a reputed shipping company with a promotion, but he wasn't sure if he was "ready." He delayed the decision. By the time he responded, the position was gone.

Months later, he was still stuck at home, waiting for another "perfect fit." He had already missed the bus. I told him, "You don't have to be 100% ready. You just need to step forward when the window opens."

That's how it works in life.

The Harbor Master's Clock

At every tidal port, there's a harbor master who sets the movement schedule. No ship, no matter how mighty, sails without aligning to that clock. In Bristol, we were 2 hours late in requesting clearance.

And that's all it took. We missed the tide by a sliver.

We didn't sail until the next afternoon. Two hours of delay cost us twenty-four hours. Ports don't bend for anyone. The sea doesn't wait. The world keeps moving.

Imagine applying that same principle to your personal life. Close your eyes for a moment and try to remember when -

- That phone call you delayed making—to apologize, to say sorry, to reconnect, to say "I love you."
- That interview you hesitated to attend.
- That fitness goal you postponed until after the holidays.
- That investment opportunity you ignored until the market changed.

Opportunities, like tides, are time-bound. They don't wait for your comfort. They wait for your courage.

A Captain's Regret

One of the most emotional conversations I've ever had happened not at sea, but on land.

It was a quiet afternoon. I was visiting a retired captain — a man who had spent over 40 years commanding ships across the globe. We sat side by side on weathered garden chairs, sipping coffee in the shadow of a home built with stories and salt.

"I've sailed through typhoons," he said, his voice steady. "I've stared down pirates, battled engines that failed in storms, and held the lives of the crew in my hands."

He paused, then looked away.

"But the hardest storm I ever faced," he continued, "was one I never expected. It wasn't at sea. It was when I came home — and realized I had waited too long to tell my wife what she meant to me."

He told me about her — a woman of quiet grace, who raised their children alone while he was away at sea for months, sometimes years. She wrote him long letters. Cooked his favorite meals when he came home. Waited at the pier without complaint, smiling every time he returned — no matter how late, no matter how tired.

"I always thought she knew," he said. "That I didn't have to say it—not in words. I showed it by providing, by being faithful, by coming home."

He sipped his coffee. His eyes, aged but clear, shimmered with unspoken weight.

"But the truth is… she needed to hear it. She needed to hear that she was more than just the anchor to my voyage — she *was* the voyage. And I never said it."

His wife had passed just two years before our conversation. Cancer — swift and cruel. He had been away on one of his final voyages when she was admitted to the hospital. He arrived just a day after the end.

"I wanted to tell, I loved her. For the first time in words." He paused. "But she was gone."

"Ships can wait for tides. But hearts… hearts can't."

His story wasn't just a memory — it was a warning.

Don't wait. Say what matters. The tide doesn't return twice.

That moment stayed with me. It pierced deeper than any storm I've faced.

As captains, as professionals, and as people, we often wait for the *perfect* moment to say what matters most. We wait for calm seas, for less stress, for the *right time*. But the tide of life doesn't wait for our hesitation.

So, if there's something you need to say — *say it.*

If there's someone you've taken for granted — *thank them.*

If there's love in your heart — *speak it.*

Because while ships can wait for high tide, hearts run on a much shorter schedule.

Say the words. Send the message. Show up — before the tide goes out.

That's not just a lesson.

That's Captain's code.

Launch When the Wind is With You

In sailing, you don't just wait for any wind—you wait for a fair wind. A headwind can delay you, but a favorable one can help you cover miles with ease. When you get that wind, you hoist the sails—immediately.

It's the same with energy, inspiration, or momentum. If you feel a surge—act.

Don't ignore the burst of motivation that says, "Start writing that book."

Don't suppress the pull in your heart that says, "Make that career switch."

Don't hold back when you feel the strength to forgive, to begin, to try.

That moment of courage is your tide. Don't let it pass.

- **The Quiet Clock of Health** One of the most deceptive tides in life is health. It ebbs quietly—often unnoticed. You feel a little tired and a bit off, but keep pushing. Then comes the diagnosis. Then the regret.

Prevention, like a tide, has a timing. Once that window closes, all you can do is wait and hope.

Don't wait. Go to the doctor. Take the walk. Say no to the third drink. Sleep.

Courage Is a Decision

Let's be clear—acting swiftly doesn't mean acting recklessly. A captain never sails without preparation. But once the conditions align, he doesn't wait for approval. He moves.

The difference between success and regret isn't always intelligence. It's an initiative.

Think of the businesses that grew because someone acted before the market changed. The relationships were saved because someone spoke up before silence became a wall. The health transformed because someone didn't wait for symptoms to worsen.

Speed doesn't mean haste. It means readiness. Response. Respect for the tide.

If you're waiting for everything to be perfect before you act, you'll miss the voyage.

Opportunities are not polite. They don't knock three times. They surge once. You either rise with them—or watch them pull away from the dock.

So, ask yourself now:

- What tide in your life is rising right now?
- What are you delaying because you're unsure or scared?
- What voyage are you meant to begin—but keep waiting on?

The captain in you already knows the answer. The sea won't wait. Neither should you.

Hoist your anchor. Raise your sail.

The tide is now.

Part 2 Storms Don't Wait for You to Be Ready — Courage Over Certainty

Readiness is a Mirage—Action Builds Clarity

People often think sea captains are fearless by nature—that we stand on the bridge with steely eyes, unmoved by the fury of nature. But that's a myth. Fear visits us, too. Sometimes it whispers, other times it roars. But over the years, we learn that fear is not a stop sign. It's a signal. A reminder to stay sharp, not to stand still.

I remember watching junior officers freeze when a sudden wave rose or an unexpected alarm pierced the silence. It wasn't weakness—it was hesitation. They were waiting for someone to say, "Now is the time to act." But at sea, time doesn't offer that luxury. The ocean doesn't knock politely; it crashes in. There is no perfect moment. There's only the moment you're in.

On land, I see the same pattern. People delay big decisions—leaving a toxic job, starting a new venture, mending a broken bond—waiting for some inner green light. They say, "I'm not ready yet." But here's the truth, drawn from my logbook of storms and stillness: clarity doesn't precede action. It follows it. I've seen nervous cadets become confident officers not because they had all the answers, but because they dared to take the first uncertain step.

You don't need to feel fearless. You just need to be willing.

Willing to try. Willing to begin. Willing to risk mistakes.

Courage is often nothing more than moving forward with shaking hands. So, if you're still waiting for a sign—this is it.

Set sail. Now.

Navigate with What You Have—Not What You Wish For

Once, on an outbound voyage from Hong Kong, we lost our GPS just as we were entering one of the busiest shipping lanes in the world. The instinct was to pause, troubleshoot, and delay. But the clock—and the current—waited for no one. We had to move. So, we relied on the oldest skills in the book: radar distances, visual bearings, manual position fix on paper charts, and instinct sharpened by years of watchkeeping.

We didn't have everything we wanted. But we had had enough. And with calm minds and steady hands, we carried on.

We wait for the stars to align—the right finances, the right time, the right mood—before we act. But life, like the sea, rarely offers perfection. It offers an opportunity. And those who wait too long risk drifting past it.

Want to start a new health habit? Repair a relationship? Launch a dream? Want to write a book? Want to start a new business? Or just want to say something to your loved one for a long time? Don't wait to have every tool in the box. Begin with what you have. Use the skills and resources within arm's reach. The rest will come as you move.

Like a good sailor, trust your instincts, adapt quickly, and stay the course.

Momentum is your friend. Stillness is not.

Courage Leaves the Harbor—Not Regret

I once faced a career-defining moment—an opportunity for promotion that I'd been dreaming of. But when it came, I hesitated. Fear clouded my vision: "What if I fail? What if I'm not good enough?"

I almost declined.

But then I remembered the tides. Unlike the tide, the opportunity will not return the next day. And the truth is that stillness breeds regret.

It's not the tempests you remember most—it's the quiet, haunting silence of chances not taken. So, I took the offer. Despite my nerves, I raised the anchor and sailed into unfamiliar waters.

That voyage changed me. Not because it was smooth, but because it demanded more of me than I knew I had.

The hardest moments in life are rarely ones we feel fully ready for. But they are the ones that show us who we really are. Don't wait for confidence. Just move with courage.

Take the first step.

If you're afraid, do it afraid. But do it.

You weren't built to be anchored. You were built to sail.

Let Courage Chart the Course

The sea never sends you a calendar invite. It shifts without warning.

We spend so much of our lives waiting—for the wind to be right, the charts to be clear, the fear to fade. But readiness is a choice, not a condition. It's that quiet voice inside that says, "I don't have all the answers, but I'm willing to begin."

Many of you want to write a book. You may have written a couple of pages and deleted them, thinking of mistakes in grammar, spelling, or simply to improve them. You have doubt in mind, who would read my book? Take the courage, write it, publish it. The moment you leave the harbor of doubt. That's the moment growth begins.

If you wait for the sea to promise smooth waters, you'll never leave shore. But if you trust your training, your instincts, and your heart, you'll find that courage to trust your compass. Not the absence of difficulty, but the willingness to face it head-on.

So, wherever you stand today—on the edge of a decision, a dream, or a storm—take the helm. **Adjust your sails. Begin your voyage. Today…and now.**

Because storms don't wait.

And neither should you.

What Storm Are You Waiting To Sail Through?

What decision have you been putting off, waiting for the "right time"?

What goal tugs at your heart but feels too risky to begin?

Are you waiting for the storm to pass, or are you ready to raise anchor and face it head-on?

Think about the tools you already possess—your past experiences, your instincts, your resilience. Could those be enough to start?

If the tide turned tomorrow, would you be ready—or would regret weigh heavier than risk?

So, ask yourself: what's one small, brave action you can take today to move forward?

Part 3: The Compass Only Works If You Move — Action Creates Direction

The Still Ship Learns Nothing

I still remember the early days of my career as a cadet of a large tanker vessel, anchored in peaceful weather at Fujairah in the United Arab Emirates. We had been waiting for orders for more than thirty days. The skies were blue, the sea calm, the crew relaxed. From the outside, it might've looked like a dream.

But I wasn't at peace. I felt a strange sense of agitation. We were on a ship equipped with modern tools a mariner could ask for— radar, satellite communication, and of course, a precision gyro compass mounted proudly at the helm.

And yet, those tools meant nothing while we were anchored. The compass needle pointed north, yes, but without movement, there was no course, no heading, no real purpose. A ship might as well be tied to the dock if it's not making way.

- That's when it struck me: even the best compass is useless if the ship isn't moving. You can't steer a parked car can you?. Navigation only begins once you're in motion.

We often wait—sometimes for too long. Waiting for the "right time," the perfect conditions, a little more certainty. But we fail to move. Life doesn't reward stillness. It rewards action.

You can't find your direction in life while anchored in place.

The Paralysis of Overthinking

We read another article, watched another video, and asked five more people for advice—all in the name of "getting ready." But readiness, like the weather, is never fully predictable.

Take my friend Ramen, for example. He spent years dreaming of launching a marine consultancy firm. He attended every seminar, made detailed business plans, and even designed a website. But he never opened the doors. He was always preparing, always waiting for the stars to align.

Meanwhile, others with half his knowledge and twice his courage stepped in and succeeded.

The truth is, clarity comes through engagement, not contemplation. The action itself is the best teacher.

You don't need a full map to begin the journey. Often, all you need is the courage to leave the harbor.

Small Steps, Significant Progress

"That's one small step for man, one giant leap for mankind."astronaut Neil Armstrong after putting his left foot on the lunar surface.

Progress doesn't require speed—it requires direction. Even if you have a one-knot speed of forward motion, you may not reach your destination quickly, but you'll be moving, correcting, and learning.

A friend of mine was trying to write her first book. For years, she had the outline, the vision, and even a publisher willing to wait. But she couldn't finish it—because she wanted it to be perfect from page one.

One day, I told her, "Just write 300 words a day. That's it. Don't worry if it's good or not. Just move."

Three months later, she had a full draft. It wasn't perfect, but it was real. From there, she could edit, polish, and publish.

You don't need giant leaps. You just need small, consistent steps.

Embracing Uncertainty

Years ago, I was offered the chance to join a maiden voyage of a new class of gantry ship, moving between the US West Coast and Japan. I'd never sailed in those types of ships. The crew was young. The technology was new. Everything about the assignment felt risky. My first instinct was to decline. I told myself I needed more time to prepare. I didn't accept those modern vessels; I lost the opportunity.

But then I remembered that still ship in the bay—and how even the best compass needs motion. So, when the opportunity came a second time, I said yes.

And it turned out to be one of the most formative experiences of my life. We faced violent storms, failures, breakdowns, and power outages—but we also discovered new efficiencies, built a solid crew bond over the years, and earned the trust of the shipping company.

I should have taken the opportunity the first time. But if I didn't take the opportunity the second time, I would've missed it all.

Growth happens when you sail beyond the sight of the shore.

The Courage to Drift Before You Steer

Sometimes we don't need a plan—we just need movement. Even a drifting vessel eventually finds the current.

I've seen many who took odd jobs, moved cities, or changed careers simply because they needed to move. And that motion, though initially unclear, brought clarity with time.

If you're unemployed, write one résumé today.

If you're lonely, talk to a friend.

If you're unhealthy, speak to a doctor.

Don't wait for a full map. Just cast off the ropes and start moving.

The compass will do its job once you're underway.

Steer Into Your Own Horizon

As I look back, I realize my life's direction was never about one perfect plan. It was about motion. About being willing to sail, even when the sky wasn't clear.

I've made mistakes. I've taken wrong turns. But I kept moving. And because of that, I found my path—not all at once, but wave by wave.

Don't wait for the storm to pass. Don't wait for perfect weather or flawless maps.

The compass is ready. It's inside you.

But it only works if you move. Move today.

Set Sail

Life is a vast ocean—beautiful, unpredictable, sometimes terrifying. And as any sailor knows, there's only one way to cross it: you have to start moving. Do not wait for anything. Let's do it today and now.

You may not know the full route. The winds may shift. The waters may rise. But as long as you keep moving, your compass will guide you.

And when you look back, you won't remember the times you waited—you'll remember the times you dared.

So, Captain, start the engine. Hoist the anchor.

Even the smallest movement can carry you toward greatness.

You cannot wait any longer.

Part 4: Small Delays, Big Consequences — The Cost of Waiting

The Silent Threats We Ignore

Small issues we spot but choose to ignore. A strange ache in the side. A rising credit card balance. An uncomfortable silence is growing in a relationship. These things don't announce themselves with sirens. They whisper, and often we pretend not to hear.

I recall a fellow mariner who began experiencing chest discomfort during his leave at home. "It's just fatigue," he said. "I'll rest and it will be all right." He delayed making an appointment with a doctor, convincing himself it was nothing. After a few weeks, he had a heart attack. Thankfully, he survived. But had he acted sooner, the outcome might have been less severe—and far less traumatic.

Waiting doesn't make a problem disappear. It allows it to grow roots. What starts as a crack in the hull becomes a flood if we wait too long.

Don't Wait to Correct Course

On the bridge, one of the most crucial rules is simple: act early. If you're heading towards danger, the earlier you correct your course, the smaller the adjustment needed. A one-degree change early on can mean miles of distance from trouble later. Wait too long, and even a hard turn might not be enough.

It's easier to cut down on sugar now than manage diabetes later.

Easier to address stress today than to face burnout tomorrow.

Easier to speak up now than to repair years of silence.

"Tide waits for none". In our personal lives, we face similar "tide moments." The opportunity to say sorry before the wound gets deeper. The moment to invest a small amount before prices soar. The chance to spend time with loved ones before time runs out.

When we delay, the consequences aren't always immediate, but they often come back around—and they're rarely easy to fix.

The Delayed Conversation

Let me share something deeply personal.

Years ago, I had a close friend—a brother in all but name. We'd shared countless memories and laughter that echoed through the years. But during a simple get-together, a disagreement flared. Pride got in the way. Words were left hanging, and we drifted apart without ever mending the bond.

I thought of calling him many times. "Next week," I'd tell myself. "When work slows down". "When the time feels right." But the days turned to months, and the silence grew like fog between two distant ships.

Then came the call I never expected.

He had passed. Cancer. Quietly. Alone.

The moment hit me like a Tsunami—sudden, shattering, and irreversible. The weight of that "calling" crushed me. Not because we had fought. But because I waited. Because I thought there'd be more time.

But the tide had already gone out.

I never got to say I was sorry. Never got to remind him that our bond was bigger than one moment of ego.

Life doesn't always offer second chances. Some ports you never reach again.

So, if there's someone in your life—a friend, a sibling, a parent, a partner, a loved one—**don't wait. Make the call. Say the words.** Drop the anchor of pride.

Because sometimes, the cost of waiting isn't delay—it's a loss that echoes forever.

Don't Wait for the Storm

As I look back on decades at sea, if there's one truth that rises above the rest, it's this: ***delay is the enemy of progress***. Ships are not built to remain in the harbor. They are meant to sail.

And sailing means making decisions—sometimes fast, sometimes with uncertainty, but always with purpose.

Don't wait for perfect conditions.

Don't wait for absolute clarity.

Don't wait for the crisis to push you.

Act now—while the skies are clear, while the winds are favorable, while you still can.

Because when the storm comes, the most prepared one survives.

And the most prepared are those who didn't wait.

Sail Now — The Tide Will Not Wait

The tide rises and falls on its own time. It doesn't wait for a captain to finish breakfast or for a ship's engine to warm up. It moves—steady, certain, and unapologetic. In life, the same rule applies. Opportunities don't wait for you to be ready. They appear, swell like the tide, and then roll away.

You don't wait for permission from the weather—you read the sky and act.

It's the same in life. Too many people stay anchored in the harbor of "someday."

Someday I'll change careers.

Someday I'll get healthy.

Someday I'll reconnect with my family.

Someday I'll write a book.

But someday is not on the calendar.

We stall because we're afraid—afraid of failure, judgment, or not having it all figured out.

I've made mistakes in my life, no doubt. I've set sail on rough waters and had to turn back. But I've never regretted starting. Regret, in my experience, is anchored in **inaction**—the job not applied for, the apology not spoken, the dream not pursued.

The key is not to have every answer. It's to move. To hoist your sails, check your compass, and begin. The course can always be corrected. But only if you're moving.

So, if you're waiting for the right time, let me tell you as a captain and as a man: **The tide won't wait.**

Sail now.

Be swift. Be bold.

Be underway.

CHAPTER 7

CALM SEAS NEVER MADE A SKILLED SAILOR – WHERE RESILIENCE IS BORN

Strength is not built in ease but in challenge. The storms of life — emotional, mental, or circumstantial — are what forge resilience, depth, and wisdom.

Part 1: Weathering the Unexpected — Strength Through Shock

The Calm Before the Chaos

IIt was winter in the North Pacific, a familiar yet unforgiving stretch of sea. Our vessel was en route from Yokohama to Los Angeles, slicing through slightly choppy waters with a confident rhythm. The bow dipped and rose, rhythmically crashing into the swell, creating towers of salt spray that glittered momentarily in the early morning light. To an untrained eye, it looked dramatic. But for us sailors, this was business as usual.

As a Chief Officer, I had already gone through our heavy weather checklist with each department. Every cargo lashing was inspected, every deck equipment secured, and every hatch double-checked. The forecast showed a low-pressure system, but it was predicted to pass around 200 nautical miles north of us—no immediate threat.

Still, our Captain was an old hand at sea and knew that the ocean had a mind of its own. He calmly ordered another round of inspections. "Double-check the cargo lashings," he said. "Make sure everything's secure." That order, which some might have seen as redundant, would turn out to be prophetic.

The Storm that Didn't Knock

I was on the bridge at 5 a.m., observing the weather and making a weather report for sending, when I felt a shift—not in the ship's direction, but in the wind's whisper. What had been a steady breeze began to growl. The gusts hit 80 knots within the next hour. In an hour, waves rose like dark walls—twenty to twenty-five feet high—pounding the hull with relentless fury.

Eventually, the storm transformed the ocean into a monstrous battlefield. Even our massive container vessel—steel giant of the sea—suddenly felt like a fragile toy tossed in the hands of a furious god. Towering waves, rising like black walls of water, surrounded us.

One moment, we were thrown atop a 30-foot crest, the horizon vanishing beneath us. The very next, we plunged into a deep trough, swallowed by darkness, with wave mountains looming on either side like watery cliffs ready to collapse. It felt as though the sea itself was trying to crush us.

With each surge, walls of water slammed the deck, ripping across the surface like claws, half-submerging the ship, and tearing at anything unsecured. The wind screamed through the masts, and the hull groaned under pressure as if the vessel itself feared what lay ahead.

At that moment, every man on board knew that this was nature at its most merciless. And we were nothing but intruders in its fury.

It hit us without warning.

The storm hadn't just veered—it had changed direction and charged straight toward us. We were directly beneath the center of the low-pressure system. The ocean, moments ago, merely rough, turned hostile. The vessel rolled and pitched violently, like a cork caught in a washing machine.

I called the Captain immediately. He arrived within minutes, calm but focused. We both stared at the updated weather chart. The system had not just altered course—it had intensified.

Chaos Below Deck

Then came the reports.

The sofa in the recreation room had ripped free and was smashing itself from wall to wall like a battering ram. In the messroom, the plate racks had broken and shattered glass and ceramic slid across the floor like a lethal tide. The messman radioed in: "It's dangerous to even walk across the room. We can't cook. Everyone's sick."

Many of the crew were violently seasick. One able-bodied seaman collapsed from exhaustion and dehydration. The Second Officer was reassigned from watchkeeping to checking in on sick and frightened crew members.

Below deck, the engine room was in turmoil. The Chief Engineer and the duty watch were in a constant fight with the main engine, which kept tripping due to unstable parameters. Every time they got it running, a massive roll would throw off the readings again.

Twenty-six hours. That's how long it lasted.

Damage Assessment

When the winds finally started to ease, we were battered, bruised, and exhausted. The vessel looked like a battlefield. I, the Chief Engineer, and a few others stepped out on deck to assess the damage. What we saw broke our hearts.

Containers had broken free. A few had split open—contents lost to the depths. The ventilation heads were torn off their mounts, and the winches were damaged beyond recognition. Sections of the ship's structure had buckled, including a cracked bulkhead that would need immediate repair at the next port.

But the most serious damage wasn't physical.

The crew was demoralized. Many were shaken to their core. A few crew members felt like near a near-death situation, and they could not come out of the shock. We hadn't eaten in 24 hours.

Everyone was tired, seasick, scared—and now had to face the cleanup and repairs.

This, right here, was the test of emotional resilience.

Shifting from Damage to Determination

With barely any rest, we had to restore functionality. We cleaned, secured, and repaired what we could. Everyone pitched in. And in those hours of post-storm hustle, a powerful transformation happened—despair gave way to determination.

Life will try to shake your core. But action—however small—restores it. The moment you start doing it, even if it's just sweeping broken glass, **you move from victim to survivor. From powerless to purposeful.**

Reflections in the Quiet

Two days later, as we neared the U.S. coastline, the sea was calm. The sun shone on the repaired deck gear. The storm had passed, but it had left its mark.

I stood alone on the bridge, sipping another cup of coffee—this one warm. I thought about how close we came to real catastrophe, and yet how we endured.

And I realized something:

The storm hadn't just tested our ship. It had tested our spirit.

The True Test Begins After the Storm

People often think the hardest part is surviving the storm. But sailors know better. The real challenge is what comes after—the rebuilding, the recovering, the restoring of normalcy.

I gathered the crew for a short meeting in the messroom, still chaotic from the damage. I looked around at their faces—pale, worn out, some with cuts and bruises. And I told them something I deeply believed:

"We faced a storm that even weather charts didn't see coming. We held our ground. Yes, we took a hit. But we're here. And we're moving forward—not just as a crew, but as a team."

Why Resilience Is Not About Toughness

There's a common myth that resilience is about being tough. But let me tell you—some of the toughest-looking crew members broke down that day. And some of the quietest, most overlooked sailors were the ones holding others up.

Resilience isn't boldness. It's adaptability. It's not about resisting the wave but adjusting your sails to ride it out.

I remember a junior cadet who spent the storm helping clean up broken dishes and comforting a crying cook who thought he had failed to feed the crew. That cadet showed me what resilience looks like—not loud, not muscular, but deeply human.

Bringing It Back to Life on Shore

Maybe you've never sailed into a Pacific storm, but I guarantee you've weathered your own. A divorce. A diagnosis. A career failure. A betrayal.

And maybe, like our ship, you came out a little damaged—scratched, bruised, shaken.

But did you survive? Yes. Are you still sailing? If you're reading this, the answer is surely yes.

The world often teaches us to avoid discomfort and to resist pain. But as sailors know, calm seas don't teach you much. It's the storm that forges you. That reveals what's inside. That shows you who you really are.

You Don't Rise—You Revert to Training

So, how do you build emotional resilience?

Not by waiting for the storm.

You build it during the calm—by nurturing mental habits, by facing smaller fears, by pushing yourself in small, meaningful ways. By talking instead of bottling it up. By setting boundaries. By taking care of your body and mind.

You prepare for the big wave by paddling every day.

When the storm hits, you won't rise magically to the occasion. You'll fall back on the habits, the mindset, the support system, and the self-belief you built when the skies were blue.

Resilience isn't avoiding storms. It's learning how to weather them. It's in how you respond, how you rebuild, and how you lead—even when your own hands are shaking.

– So, train your heart Not for calm seas—but for the next wave.

Part 2: The Bilge Below — Handling Emotional Buildup

The Hidden Part of the Ship

If you've ever stepped below deck on a ship, beyond the humming engine room and clattering machinery, you'll find a place few talk about but every sailor knows well—the bilge. It's dark, damp, and smells of oil and rust. This is where all the unwanted stuff collects: stray seawater, leaking oil, bits of waste, and leftover residue from the ship's daily workings.

Nobody celebrates the bilge. But everyone respects it.

Because if you ignore it, it becomes a slow, silent killer.

If the bilge overflows, then it is a sign of danger. It's a sign of leakage or machinery malfunctions. A ship can be polished topside, but if her bilge is neglected, disaster is just a matter of time.

And that, my friend, is exactly how emotions work.

Beneath Our Own Decks

In life, we all have our own "emotional bilge." These are the feelings we don't want to deal with—resentment from an old betrayal, an ego clash with a close friend, grief from a loss we never processed, guilt we carry quietly, anger we swallowed years ago.

We don't like to acknowledge these things. Like bilge water, they're messy, smelly, and feel inconvenient.

But pretending they aren't there doesn't make them go away. Just like a ship's bilge, they keep collecting—bit by bit, day by day.

I remember a young Chief Officer I once sailed with. Bright, hardworking, polite. But over time, I noticed he would snap over small things—if a wrench wasn't in place, if someone forgot to greet him, if a junior made an honest mistake. His anger wasn't about the moment—it was overflowing.

One evening during watch, I asked him gently, "What's really bothering you?"

He broke down, right there on the bridge. He told me he had lost his father six months ago, just before joining the ship.

"I didn't want to seem weak," he said. "So, I never told anyone. There is a lot of burden on me, I just… kept going."

But emotions don't just go away because we ignore them. They wait, quietly, in the bilge of our minds. And when the pressure gets too high, they burst through the seams.

Every Ship Has Bilge — and So Do We

It's important to know that emotional build-up is not a failure. It's part of being human.

Even the most advanced, well-maintained ship in the world still collects water in its bilge. That doesn't mean it's a bad ship. It just means it's operating.

You're not broken because you feel grief, guilt, or sadness. You're not weak because you're overwhelmed. You're alive. And you're navigating life, which—like the ocean—is vast and often unpredictable.

But just as every good sailor respects their bilge, every wise person respects their emotions.

Cleaning the Bilge

The bilge needs to be cleaned. It's a routine. Because maintenance is prevention.

We need the same habits for our minds.

That doesn't mean breaking down every day or living in our feelings. It means finding healthy ways to release emotional build-up—before it corrodes us.

For some, it's journaling—just writing out what's going on inside without judgment. For others, it's talking to a friend, or a therapist, or even taking long walks alone and letting the mind breathe, spending time with yourself.

A few drops of stress here, a few drops of bitterness there, an unresolved argument with someone close, a silent wound—and one day, the alarm goes off. Maybe in the form of burnout. Maybe a relationship collapses. Maybe your health suffers.

The tragedy isn't the breakdown. It's that we saw it coming, and we didn't act – we remained silent.

"I'll deal with this later."

"It's not a big deal."

"I should be strong enough to handle it."

But strength isn't suppression. Strength is knowing when to pump the bilge.

One of the most dangerous myths in life is that "time heals all wounds."

Time only buries them. It's what you do with that time that heals.

How to Pump Your Emotional Bilge

Ask honestly: "Is there anything building up inside?"

If there is, name it. That's the first rule of emotional bilge maintenance—**name the feeling**. Anger. Shame. Envy. Sadness.

Don't hide it behind jokes, workaholism, or silence. Give it a name. That's how you take away its power.

Here are a few tools I've learned from life at sea and from mentoring young crew:

- **Name the Feeling**: When something doesn't feel right, ask yourself—What am I really feeling? Be honest. Anger is often sadness in armor. Guilt might be masking helplessness.
- **Talk It Out**: Speak to someone. A friend, mentor, therapist, or even a colleague. Speaking the truth out loud often shrinks its weight.
- **Journal Without Editing**: Don't worry about grammar or structure. Just let your thoughts flow onto paper or a diary, or just list out a few points in your notebook. You'd be amazed at how much lighter you feel.
- **Move Your Body**: Physical movement releases trapped emotional energy. A walk, a run, or even 15 minutes of stretching can make a big difference.
- **Find Stillness**: Whether through meditation, prayer, or quiet reflection—stillness allows the silt to settle and clarity to rise.

The Strength in Letting Go

One day after anchoring at Port Klang, I was speaking to a seasoned Bosun who had sailed for nearly 40 years. I asked him how he stayed calm.

He smiled and said, "I don't hold onto what I don't need. That's the secret. On every voyage, I let something go. Otherwise, my ship gets heavy."

That stayed with me.

In life, we all carry more than we need. **Regrets we can't change. Hurts we never deserved. Words we wish we could take back.** But your soul—like your ship—needs to stay light if you want to keep sailing.

So don't wait for the alarm to go off.

Pump your bilge.

Release the buildup.

Let go of what no longer serves you.

Because peace isn't found by patching the surface. It's earned by cleaning what lies beneath.

Mental resilience is not about pretending everything is fine.

It's about being brave enough to face what's not.

Clean out your emotional bilge before it corrodes your core.

Let your heart sail free.

Part 3: Holding the Helm in Chaos — The Power of Steady Focus

It isn't Strength —It's Focus

People often think steering a vessel through a storm is about muscle. But the truth is, physical strength means nothing when your environment is unpredictable. One wrong move, one overcorrection, and the ship can broach sideways, exposing herself to the full fury of the sea.

You don't fight the storm. You work with it.

You respond to each wave with presence, with grace. You don't grip the wheel tighter—you steady your breath. Your hands don't grip—they listen. Focus is what keeps the course. Focus is what gets you through.

Some storms test a ship's design. And then, some storms test the sailor's soul.

The Chaos in Life Is No Different

Life has its own storms. Some arrive with a warning; others crash in unannounced. You may lose a job overnight. A loved one may fall sick. A relationship may loosen up. A heartbreak. An accident. Finances nosedive; you name it. Your inner peace may be shaken by nothing more than a string of small disappointments, piled high and unnoticed.

In these moments, panic is the easiest reaction.

We start grasping for control over things we cannot command. We obsess over what others did wrong, what should've happened, and what we wish we could undo. Our thoughts scatter like loose cargo in a rolling hold. Like at sea, you cannot control a moving cargo when the vessel is rolling and pitching heavily in rough weather.

But panic doesn't help.

Focus does.

Focus: Your Emotional Rudder

Imagine you're standing on the bridge of your life-ship in a personal storm. Waves of uncertainty crash over you. The radar's unclear. The horizon is hidden. What do you do?

You go back to the basics.

You focus on what *you* can control.

In a storm, I can't stop the waves. But I can control the ship's heading. I can adjust the speed. I can read the instruments, issue commands, and ensure my crew is safe.

In life, I can't stop the heartbreak.

Whether it's the loss of a loved one, the end of a relationship, or the betrayal of trust—heartbreak comes like a rogue wave. You don't see it coming until you're already gasping for air.

Heartbreak is real. It hurts. It cracks open the hull and lets in silence, regret, and sorrow. But you have a choice. You can let the pain define your voyage—or you can navigate through it.

Start by acknowledging the pain. Don't shove it into the bilge of your heart where it'll rust your spirit. Talk. Write. Walk. Weep if you must. Every storm has a cycle—and so does grief.

Next, focus on what's still intact. Hold tight to your values, your people, and your purpose. Let what remains give you strength.

Finally, steer forward. It doesn't mean forgetting. It means honoring what was and choosing to live well anyway. The sea always opens up again. New stars appear. Calm eventually returns.

You can't outrun heartbreak. But you can endure it.

And when you do, you're not broken. You're seasoned.

You can decide whether to be reactive or reflective.

You can anchor yourself in the moment and navigate the hour—not the week, not the year—just the hour.

That is the focus. That is power.

The Power of Small, Controlled Actions

During that storm, we cannot focus on how long the storm will last or how much damage we might suffer. Instead, we focused on the next swell, the next 10 seconds, and the next course correction.

That's what life asks of us, too.

You don't need to solve everything at once. Just focus on the next right thing.

If your heart is broken, don't try to fix your future. Calm down. Drink some water. Call a friend. Take a walk. Weep if you need to.

If your finances are in shambles, don't try to become a millionaire overnight. Just make a list. Cancel an unnecessary expense. Write down your income and expenses. Make a budget to stay within your earnings. Save, even if it is small, forcefully.

One small action at a time. That's the sailor's way.

A Calm Mind Is Your Rudder

Ships are designed to handle more than we think. But only if we steer with focus.

Sometimes, chaos isn't outside—it's within.

You might look calm on the surface, but feel like you're spiraling inside. Thoughts racing. Emotions crashing. Doubt thick like fog.

This is where holding the helm of the *mind* becomes critical.

Steady focus doesn't mean having no fear. It means moving through fear with attention. It means not letting the loudest thought take control. It means asking, "What's the *next best* thing I can do?"—not the perfect one, not the easy one, just the next best one.

"Weren't you afraid?"

"Yes. But fear is allowed. Losing focus isn't."

That's the lesson I want to leave with you.

You don't need to be fearless.

You just need to be *focused.*

When the world rages around you, don't try to control it.

Control your steering.

Focus on the next action.

The next breath.

The next step.

Storms will come. But they also pass.

And if you hold the helm steady,

You will always find your way home.

Part 4: Battle-Tested — Turning Scars into Strength

There's a quiet truth every seasoned mariner knows but rarely speaks aloud: the strongest ships are not the ones that look perfect. They're the oncs that have survived storms and still sail forward—marked, repaired, and battle-tested.

Scars Tell a Story

Isn't life like that?

We all carry damage. Sometimes, it's visible—like wrinkles from years of worry or scars from physical injuries. But often, it's hidden deep inside—heartbreak from a relationship that broke your spirit, a failure that wounded your confidence, a betrayal that shook your trust.

These emotional scars, like dents in a ship's hull, can make us feel vulnerable and broken.

But here's what sailing has taught me: damage doesn't mean you're done. In fact, if addressed properly, that damage becomes your strength.

You patch. You reinforce. And you keep moving.

Your emotional scars are proof you've sailed through storms—and survived.

Strength Through the Struggle

The crew that patched the ship that day didn't just fix steel—they found pride in their ability to adapt and overcome. I watched friendships deepen. I saw mutual respect grow. And I realized: it wasn't the good times that built our crew—it was the hardship.

Now I will tell you to think about your own emotional journey. The heartbreak that left you crying into your pillow. The business deal that collapsed after years of effort. The betrayal by someone you trusted completely. Those weren't just losses—they were moments that taught you what matters. Who matters? And most importantly, what *you're made of.*

Scars don't weaken you. They toughen you. They show where life hit you hardest—and where you stood back up.

The Fear of Being "Damaged"

Society portrays false ideas we need to be flawless to be valuable.

We edit our photos, hide our pain, and wear our smiles like armor. Aren't we? But perfection isn't strength—it's an illusion.

In relationships, we often hesitate to show our scars. We fear rejection. We fear being seen as "too broken." But the true connection doesn't come from perfection—it comes from authenticity.

When you show your scars, you're not showing weakness. You're showing history. Depth. Wisdom.

You're saying, "I've been through something—and I've lived to tell the tale."

Life's Repair Crew

After we made the permanent hull repairs in the next port, the welding team foreman said. "The patch reinforces it beyond original strength."

When we *work* through our emotional wounds—if we do not ignore them, hide them—we become stronger than before. When we seek help, talk about it, reflect, and learn—we reinforce our character.

Support systems are your friends; that's the easiest one you can fall back to. If you haven't acquired any or you have slowly drifted away from them over a period of time, you become lonely. If so, you still have mentors, therapists, and communities—they are like life's repair crew. They help us weld our cracks. But the key is letting them know. Allowing yourself to admit, "Yes, I was damaged—but I want to heal stronger."

Healing doesn't mean erasing the past. It means building on it.

Making Meaning from the Storm

One of my junior officers once came to me after a rough week. He'd lost a close friend back home and was struggling to stay focused onboard. "Sir," he said quietly, "I don't know how to keep going. I just feel... hollow."

I didn't offer him a grand lecture. Instead, I shared the story of that damaged hull. I told him how we assessed it. Faced it. Fixed it. Reinforced it.

"You don't need to be okay right now," I said. "You just need to stay afloat, and when you're ready, patch the hull. Strengthen what was broken."

Over the months that followed, I watched him do exactly that. He journaled. Spoke with the family. Threw himself into his work. Bit by bit, he came back—not the same as before, but wiser. Stronger.

That's the power of turning scars into strength.

Battle-tested and Still Sailing

In life, the most compassionate ones have known pain. The most resilient ones have faced failure. The most grounded ones have walked through storms—and kept walking.

You, too, if reading this chapter, are battle-tested.

Whatever you've survived—loss, heartbreak, fear, failure—it didn't break you, and that's why you are reading this book today. It shaped you.

And now you sail with reinforced steel, deeper wisdom, and a steadier hand on the helm.

Don't hide your scars. Wear them.

They're not signs of weakness—they are the medals life pinned on you for surviving. For showing up. For growing.

And now, you're not just sailing.

You're *leading others* through their storms.

Because you know something they haven't experienced yet:

"The ship may get damaged, but with care, courage, and character—it can sail stronger, smarter, and longer than ever."

The Sea Doesn't Give Strength — It Reveals It

You don't become a sailor by reading books in the harbor.

You become one by stepping out, hoisting the anchor, and meeting the sea head-on—with its calm sunrises and brutal tempests alike. That's where true strength is revealed—not at the dock, but in the deep.

Heartbreak, failure, betrayal—none of these things come to destroy you. They come to *introduce you* to who you really are beneath the surface.

Don't wish for an easy voyage. Easy seas make soft sailors.

Wish instead for the courage to face the storms—and the wisdom to grow from them.

Because one day, you will look back not at how smooth your life was—but at how you sailed through the rough patches. That's the measure of strength. That's the story worth telling.

And Captain, I repeat:

You were never made for the harbor.

You were made for the open sea – to face the deadliest storm.

LEAVE A WAKE WORTH FOLLOWING

Leave a Legacy Beyond the Horizon

A Captain's Final Log and Your Call to Legacy

Every ship, no matter how grand or humble, leaves a wake behind it. A ripple in the water that stretches far beyond sight. And so does every life.

As a Master Mariner who has navigated oceans, storms, calm waters, and countless ports, I tell you this: it's not how fast you sail or how shiny your ship appears that defines your legacy. It's the wake you leave — the life trail you carve through your choices, your principles, and your courage.

In this final chapter, we draw the map back to the beginning, reviewing the seven sea lessons that brought you here — and then push forward, past the visible horizon, to one question:

What will your wake look like?

Set Your True North — The Legacy of Purpose

Your legacy begins with direction. In Chapter 1, we learned that wealth alone doesn't make life rich. A richer life starts with clarity — knowing what truly matters to you. It's different for every person. Figure it out.

We began with a rescue — a life pulled from icy waters. That moment, raw and unforgettable, reminded us that richness isn't always in a paycheck. Sometimes, it's in the heartbeat you helped save, the company shared, the purpose felt deep in your chest.

This chapter was your wake-up call — not to chase wealth blindly, but to define what "rich" truly means in the context of your own life.

Your True North isn't given to you. You must choose it.

You've now seen that money alone doesn't make a rich life. A rank, a position, a house—these are just containers. What matters is what you fill them with: purpose, peace, pride, and presence.

So, here's your Captain's call:

Define your True North. What gives you meaning beyond money? What legacy do you wish to leave?

Plot your course. Don't just react to life—navigate it. Know your values, chart your goals, and prepare for storms.

Drop your anchor when needed—but don't stay stuck. The rest is good. Fear-driven paralysis is not.

The compass only works if you move. And the sea doesn't wait for those who hesitate.

Your True North is your guiding purpose. It's the legacy blueprint that shapes every decision, every relationship, and every chapter you write. Without it, you drift. With it, you sail with conviction.

Will people remember your title — or your values?

Will your children recall your possessions — or your presence?

Your True North isn't what you achieve. It's what you inspire. It's the consistent compass bearing that others can follow — even when you're no longer there.

Now is the time. Take the helm. Own your journey.

Because the voyage to a richer life begins not with more wealth—but with deeper clarity.

Steady as she goes, Captain. Your True North is calling.

Set your course. Leave a direction worth following.

Navigate by the Stars — The Legacy of Living Fully

In Chapter 2, we looked up — not to escape, but to align. Your inner talents, your quiet joys, your persistent passions — these are your stars. They are not random. They form constellations — a life pattern that no one else can replicate.

In this chapter, we left the compass behind and looked skyward — toward the timeless stars that have guided sailors for centuries. When the sea is uncertain and maps fail, true mariners look up. And when life becomes unclear, so should you.

Your stars are not in the sky — they are within you. Your passions, values, talents, and quiet strengths — these are your personal constellations. They don't scream for attention, but they are always shining. You must simply look up and look inward.

We explored how to identify your "Polaris" — your core value, the one thing that never moves, no matter how rough the voyage becomes. We talked about constellations — the patterns of your strengths — and the "sextant" of self-reflection that helps you measure how far you've come. We saw how every delay, every challenge, and even the darkest nights reveal more of who we truly are.

Most importantly, we learned that life isn't about the destination—it's about the joy of the voyage. The port isn't the point. The journey is.

What made your eyes light up as a child? What talents have you left unused? What beauty have you stopped noticing?

So, here's your captain's command:

- Stop waiting for perfect clarity. The stars don't move to suit you—you align yourself to them.
- Start small. Take a step guided by your own light. One act of courage. One honest reflection. One quiet joy.
- Let go of comparison. Stars don't compete. They shine.

The sea of life is vast. But you are not lost.

You were born with stars of your own.

So, lift your head. Trust your light. And sail on — not by fear, but by starlight.

The sky is waiting.

So is your richest life.

To leave a wake worth following, you must enjoy the journey — not just grind toward the finish. Your ability to live with wonder, gratitude, and curiosity becomes a living lighthouse to others.

Let your life say, "I didn't just survive the voyage. I danced under the stars."

Read the Wind, Adjust the Sails — The Legacy of Adaptability

The wind never stays the same. In Chapter 3, we learned that adaptability is not weakness — it is wisdom in motion.

Those who read the wind, trim the sails, and stay alert to change — they reach far shores.

Adaptability is not weakness; it's wisdom. It's the ability to pivot when plans collapse, to anticipate before the skies darken, and to make small adjustments that prevent massive derailments. Whether it's adjusting a career path, repairing a strained relationship, tightening your financial habits, or tending to your emotional well-being, the most successful people don't fight change. They flow with it.

When the wind shifts, the Captain trims the sails, reinforces the deck, checks the rudder, and keeps moving. That's your task now. Be proactive, not reactive. Don't wait for a crisis to make your move. Practice small corrections daily. Stay aware, stay responsive.

You are the captain of your life. The wind may howl, the tides may turn, but the helm is still in your hands.

Now ask yourself:

- What small adjustment can I make today?
- Where am I resisting necessary change?
- How can I prepare better for the next storm?

The seas will always shift — that's a promise. Your job is not to resist the wind but to read it, adjust your sails, and stay the course.

So, take a breath. Grip the wheel.

And sail on — wiser, stronger, and ready for whatever the horizon brings.

Your legacy isn't in pretending life didn't shake you. It's in how you responded. Did you adjust with grace? Did you shift your career, mend a broken bond, or admit when it was time to pivot?

You leave a wake of adaptability when others say, "He never quit — he adjusted and sailed on."

Life will throw squalls. Your legacy is your response.

Maintain the Hull Before It Leaks — The Legacy of Habits

Strong ships don't stay strong by accident. In Chapter 4, we dove deep into maintenance — the quiet, daily checks that keep everything afloat.

The most dangerous leaks on a ship are the ones you don't see—until it's too late. The same is true in life.

This chapter brought you into the underbelly of the ship: the engine room, the main engine, the machinery, the fuel lines, and the rusty bolts. Places that are hot, gritty, unglamorous—and vital. You've now seen that it's not the grand decisions but the daily discipline that keeps a vessel afloat. And it's not the storms that destroy us—it's the neglected cracks that grow in silence.

We walked through real stories of danger averted—not by luck, but by regular inspection. We explored how rust never sleeps, how emotional and financial corrosion sneak in, and how preventive maintenance—of both ship and self—is the secret to strength.

And when it's time to truly rest, we don't push harder—we go into dry dock. Because even the strongest vessels need time off the water. So do you.

You may be admired for your strength today. But your true legacy depends on what you do every day — when no one is watching. Your health routines, your finances, your mental habits, your spiritual alignment — they form the integrity of your hull.

Neglected, they'll crack. But nurtured, they carry you across oceans.

Are you building a life that lasts?

Are you tending to the little things that matter — the morning rituals, the sincere apologies, the thoughtful savings, the ten minutes of presence with your children?

So, here's your captain's call to action:

- Do your daily rounds. Ask yourself: "What small issue am I ignoring today that could become tomorrow's crisis?"
- Respect your engine room. Care for your health, your finances, your mindset—even if no one sees it. That's where real strength is born.
- Schedule your dry dock. Don't wait for burnout. Create a structured space for rest, reflection, and renewal.
- Stop glamorizing chaos. Routine isn't boring—it's brilliant. It's what lets you explore, take risks, and live boldly.

You are the Captain of your ship. But your habits are the hull. Tend to them daily, and no storm will shake you. Neglect them—and the sea will teach you hard lessons.

Now go. Inspect. Repair. Strengthen. Your next voyage depends on it.

Always Have a Lifeboat — The Legacy of Preparedness

No one lives storm-free. That's why Chapter 5 taught us that backup plans aren't signs of fear — they're signs of wisdom.

Life, like the sea, is unpredictable. And just as every seaworthy ship is equipped with lifeboats, your life needs its own forms of backup—emotionally, financially, and spiritually. This chapter anchored that truth deeply.

We learned that real preparation starts before the storm, not during it. Lifeboats are not mounted during chaos—they're checked weekly, drilled monthly, and trusted always. That's the mindset we must adopt in our lives: build your safety nets before you need them.

Whether it's an emergency fund, insurance policy, support network, or a coping ritual—these are your lifeboats. You may not use them every day, but when the storm comes—and it will—they're what keeps you afloat.

Financial drills simulate job loss or a crisis. Emotional drills build resilience before heartbreak strikes. Redundancy in income and emotional support from friends ensures you're not left adrift if one system fails. And most crucially, we must not ignore the early whispers of distress—in our wallets or our hearts. The earlier we act, the easier it is to recover.

As your Captain, I again remind you: hope is not a strategy. A lifeboat is.

So, here's your call to action—today. Check your lifeboat. Inspect your finances. Strengthen your relationships. Practice your coping rituals. Back up your life like you would a ship bound for unknown seas.

When the storm comes—and it will—you won't panic. You won't drown.

You'll float. Not because the sea was kind, but because you were ready.

That's the Captain's Code.

When the emergency strikes — a job loss, a sudden illness, a personal loss — will your crew know what to do? Will your family have the tools? Will you?

You leave a legacy not just by being strong in calm, but by being ready in chaos.

Have you built emotional reserves? Financial lifeboats? Support systems?

Your legacy is not "He never faced hardship." It's "When hardship came, he had already prepared. And because of him, we stayed afloat."

There Is No Tomorrow — The Legacy of Timely Action

In Chapter 6, the tide taught us its most unforgiving lesson: it waits for no one.

Life, like the sea, doesn't operate on your comfort. It runs on tide, wind, and time—forces that won't pause for hesitation. In this chapter, you've learned a sailor's deepest truth: miss the tide, miss the voyage.

We explored the cost of waiting—whether it's delaying a health check, stalling on a life decision, or hesitating to make a change you know is needed. The sea doesn't reward the most intelligent sailor. It rewards the most responsive one—the one who acts when the window opens, even if the skies aren't fully clear.

You've seen real sea stories—of storms that didn't wait, of opportunities lost in hesitation, and of vessels that stayed docked too long. And through each story, the lesson echoed loud and clear:

Waiting doesn't protect you—it costs you.

You don't need perfect certainty—you need the courage to move.

So, here's your Captain's call:

- Stop waiting for the "right time"—there isn't one.
- Set your course with what you know—and trust your compass to guide you as you go.
- Speak the words you've been holding for long. Make the move you've been delaying.
- Begin now. Because regret is a storm that hits harder than failure.

Ships are built to sail, not stay safe in port.

And you? You're not here to linger.

You're here to voyage.

The tide is rising.

Raise your anchor. Hoist your sail. Go.

Because there is no tomorrow.

Too many lives are lived on the docks of "someday." Someday I'll apologize. Someday I'll start that dream. Someday, I'll take my health seriously. But someday isn't a day on any calendar. Someday never comes.

Your legacy will never be written in your intentions — only your actions.

Don't wait to start becoming who you're meant to be. Don't let fear keep you in port. Don't let comfort rob you of courage.

You only leave a wake when you launch.

Move. Act. Speak. Begin.

Because no tide ever waited for a sailor to feel ready.

Calm Seas Never Made a Skilled Sailor — The Legacy of Resilience

This may be the most human legacy of all: showing others how to survive and grow from hardship.

In Chapter 7, we saw that resilience is not built in peace. It is built in pain. The broken hull was repaired and strengthened. The shaken crew pulled together. The scarred officer later leads with modesty and strength.

True strength isn't born in comfort—it's forged in chaos.

In this powerful chapter, I took you into the belly of the storm—not just the ones that batter ships, but the ones that batter the soul. We witnessed the fury of an unexpected tempest at sea and the emotional aftermath that tested our crew—not in the moment of crisis, but in the hours that followed. That's where resilience lives—not in surviving, but in recovering.

We descended into the emotional bilge, the unseen space below deck where residue collects. This chapter taught us that those emotions—like resentment, grief, or guilt—must be released regularly, or they corrode the core. We stood at the helm in chaos, learning that focus, not force, is what holds the ship steady. And we discovered the quiet nobility of scars—proof not of weakness, but of experience, growth, and survival.

Storms don't break a sailor—they reveal them. They strip away illusions and uncover the strength we didn't know we had.

What storms have you survived? Have you hidden your scars — or shared them as signs of hope?

Your resilience tells your children, your friends, and the world: you can face the storm, and you can rise after it.

Your legacy is not your perfection. It's your persistence.

Captain's Call to Action:

- Don't wish for easier days. Train your mind for stronger ones.
- Clean your emotional bilge—often and without shame.
- Hold the wheel steady—not with fear, but with focus.

- And most of all: honour your scars. They're not signs of damage—they're medals of resilience.

You weren't built for calm harbors.

You were made for the open sea.

Now sail—battle-tested, wiser, and unstoppable.

Final Log Entry — Leave a Wake Worth Following

Every sailor knows: when the ship has passed, what remains is the wake — a sign it was there, that it moved, that it made an impact.

The question is not whether your life will leave a wake. It's what kind of wake you will leave.

Will your wake lift others — or leave them lost in your churn?

Will it lead to light — or fade into fog?

Will it stay silent — or roar with courage?

In the end, your legacy is not a building. Not a bank account. Not a title.

Your legacy is the life you lived in full view of others:

- How you showed up.
- How you endured.
- How you grew.
- How you gave.

You are not just a sailor on this voyage of your life. You are a beacon for those who follow.

So, find your True North.

Enjoy the journey.

Trim your sails often.

Check your hull daily.

Keep your lifeboat ready.

Move with urgency.

Steady yourself in storms.

And as you go — shine.

Not for show. But to guide others to steer by your light.

Because long after you've reached your final port, your wake will stretch behind you — across generations, across hearts, across time.

That's what it means to leave a wake worth following.

That's the Captain's Code.

And now — it's all yours.

So, sail on, Captain.

Beyond the horizon — and into history.

ACKNOWLEDGEMENT

First and foremost, I offer my deepest gratitude to God for blessing me with the strength, clarity, and inspiration to bring this book to life.

This journey would not have been possible without the unwavering support of my friends and fellow mariners. Your encouragement was the wind in my sails, pushing me to pen down the lessons the sea has so patiently taught me over the years.

A special note of heartfelt thanks goes to **Professor Raja Chakraborty**. Years ago, his genuine belief in my voice as a writer sparked a journey I hadn't yet imagined. Without his early encouragement, this book may never have been written.

I am also immensely grateful to my childhood friend, **Indrajit Mukherjee**, who has been my go-to technical anchor. From helping me with Kindle Direct Publishing to resolving countless tech hurdles, his guidance and motivation have been invaluable.

Appreciation is extended to **Mr Jatin Gupta**, whose guidance, and steady support played a key role in shaping this book's creation.

Finally, to **you, my readers** thank you for choosing this book and stepping aboard the journey toward a richer life. May these seven sea lessons leave a lasting impact. If this book resonates with you, please leave your review on Amazon your words may just inspire the next readers to begin their voyage.

With warmth and gratitude,

Utpal Haldar

e-mail: utpalh@rediffmail.com
Facebook: https://www.facebook.com/utpal.haldar.5/
Instagram: https://www.instagram.com/utpalhaldar71/
LinkedIn: https://www.linkedin.com/in/utpal-haldar-49432
2234/